BASICS DESIGN

02

Layout

Ambrose / Harris

An AVA Book
Published by AVA Publishing SA
Rue des Fontenailles 16, Case postale,
1000 Lausanne 6, Switzerland
Tel: +41 786 005 109 Email: enquiries@avabooks.ch

Distributed by Thames & Hudson (ex-North America)
181a High Holborn, London WC1V 7QX, United Kingdom
Tel: +44 20 7845 5000 Fax: +44 20 7845 5055
Email: sales@thameshudson.co.uk
www.thamesandhudson.com

Distributed in the USA and Canada by:
Watson-Guptill Publications
770 Broadway, New York, NY 10003
Fax: +1 646 654 5487 Email: info@watsonguptill.com
www.watsonguptill.com

English Language Support Office
AVA Publishing (UK) Ltd.
Tel: +44 1903 204 455 Email: enquiries@avabooks.co.uk

ISBN 2-940373-34-5 / 978-2-940373-34-5
10 9 8 7 6

Design and text by Gavin Ambrose and Paul Harris
Original photography by Xavier Young
www.xavieryoung.co.uk

Production by AVA Book Production Pte. Ltd., Singapore
Tel: +65 6334 8173 Fax: +65 6259 9830 Email: production@avabooks.com.sg

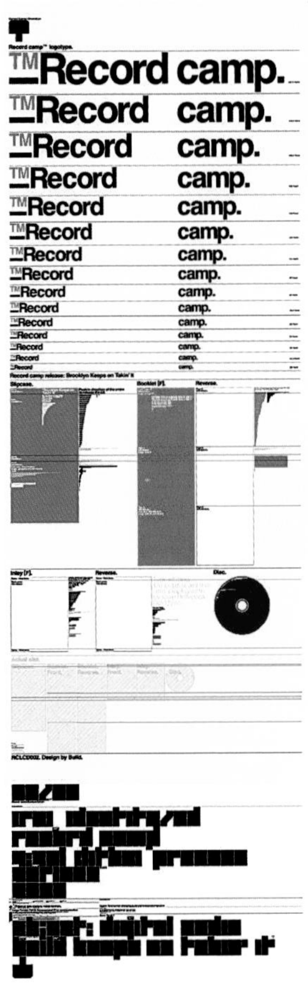

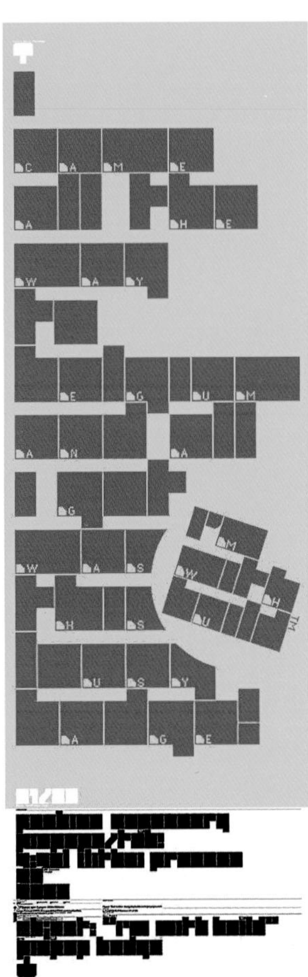

Client: DotForwardslashOffline
Design: Build
Layout synopsis:
Vertical-module structure, simple hierarchy

Computerlove

These banners were designed by Build for the Computerlove International Graphic Design Exhibition. All banners are large-format prints at 140cm x 400cm.

(left to right) The first banner is for the Record camp song *Brooklyn Keeps on Takin' It*, the middle banner is for the Pinpop remix and says 'I came all the way to Belgium and all I got was this lousy badge!' and the third banner is for the Refill Mag remix.

The exaggerated format of the banners implies a vertical-module structure; a series of distinct blocks stacked on top of one another. By occupying the main central panel with key graphic elements and supporting information resting below, a simple hierarchy is established.

Contents

North

Form Design

NB: Studio

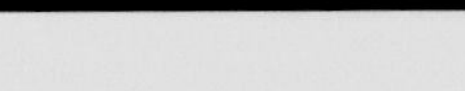

Aboud Sodano

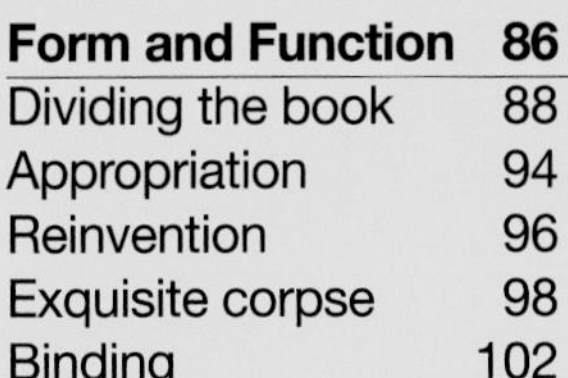

SEA Design

Studio Myerscough

Introduction

Layout concerns the placement of text and image elements within a design. How these elements are positioned, both in relation to one another and within the overall design scheme, will affect how the content is viewed and received by the readers, as well as their emotional reaction towards it. Layout can help or hinder the receipt of the information presented in a work. Similarly creative layouts can add value and embellishment to a piece, whereas understated layout can allow the content to shine through.

This book introduces the basic principles of layout as used in contemporary design. Many of these principles date back decades, and some are even centuries old although arguably in less rigorous use since the advent of desktop publishing. These basic working structures offer a number of distinct benefits as an alternative to the 'out-of-a-tin' formula that modern computer programs offer. Through the considered application of these basics a more balanced and effective layout can be achieved.

In this volume commercial projects, produced by leading contemporary design studios, showcase the intricacies and beauty of designs based on considered application (or disregard), of basic layout principles – rather than the prescriptive defaults offered by the computer.

The Basics

Here we present the fundamental layout principles and guidelines for placing elements within a design, and discuss the use of different grids as well as the anatomy of the page.

The Grid

Different treatments can produce a variety of results for text- or image-heavy designs. The examples shown here demonstrate this and present alternative options for typographical elements.

Elements on a Page

This chapter explores the relationship between the grid and the placement of text and images.

Form and Function

The intention of a project, or the specifics of a brief, will affect layout decisions. This chapter presents layout variations as well as different format and finishing options.

Layout in Use

Different types of content will have different layout and structuring requirements. In this chapter considerations such as orientation, juxtaposing and division of the page space are discussed.

Breaking the Rules

What happens to the placement of text and image elements if a designer abandons the grid? Here we see new structure can be maintained or forsaken.

Client: Fry Art Gallery
Design: Webb & Webb
Layout synopsis: Simple text treatment, image predominance

Design

Design, was produced in conjunction with an exhibition that featured works produced by artists invited by the government to record the events along the procession route of the 1953 coronation of Queen Elizabeth II.

Webb & Webb's design for the book uses a layout that is sympathetic to the historic nature of its content, with text presented so simply that attention remains focused on the images. The text block rests centrally on the page, framed by the running head at the top and the folio number mirroring this central position at the bottom of the page.

How to get the most out of this book

This book introduces different aspects of layout design via dedicated chapters for each topic. Each chapter provides numerous examples of creative layout use in design from leading contemporary design studios, annotated to explain the reasons behind the design choices made.

Key design principles are isolated so that the reader can see how they are applied in practice.

Clear navigation
Each chapter has a clear strapline for the rapid location of areas of interest.

Introductions
Special section introductions outline the basic concepts that will be discussed.

Juxtaposition

148 **149**

Juxtaposition
Juxtaposition is the deliberate placement of contrasting images side by side. The word is formed from the Latin 'juxta', which means near, and 'position'.

In graphic design and page layout juxtaposition may be used to present two or more ideas so as to impart a relationship between them, as seen in the example opposite. Here, the relationship concerns the shape of the two objects and the sensation their position suggests.

Juxtaposition may imply similarity or dissimilarity, demonstrating that two things are essentially the same or quite different. This may only be clear from the context of the work as a whole. Many designers use juxtaposition in their work with the implicit intention that readers work out the connection themselves.

Sensation (right)
This poster for the *Sensation* exhibition at the Royal Academy of Arts in London was designed by Why Not Associates and is a simple juxtaposition of two images that ordinarily do not belong together. The tongue and iron have similar shapes, but there is more at work here. The tongue appears to be touching the iron; this would cause a painfully hot sensation if the iron were switched on and so we may recoil in discomfort at the idea the image suggests by association. *Sensation* featured many controversial, contemporary art works and therefore the poster suggests the extreme nature of some of the exhibits.

Layout Layout in Use

Client: Royal Academy of Arts
Design: Why Not Associates
Layout synopsis: Juxtaposition of two images to suggest sensation

ROYAL ACADEMY OF ARTS
YOUNG BRITISH ARTISTS FROM THE SAATCHI COLLECTION
SENSATION

Impart
Ideas can be expressed implicitly or they can be suggested (or imparted) through the presentation of information that the reader decodes in order to arrive at the required interpretation. In the example above, a juxtaposition of two images is used to impart the idea of sensation.

Layout Juxtaposition

Written explanations
Key points are explained within the context of an example project.

Examples
Commercial projects from contemporary designers bring the principles under discussion alive.

Diagrams

Diagrams add meaning to theory by showing the basic principles in action.

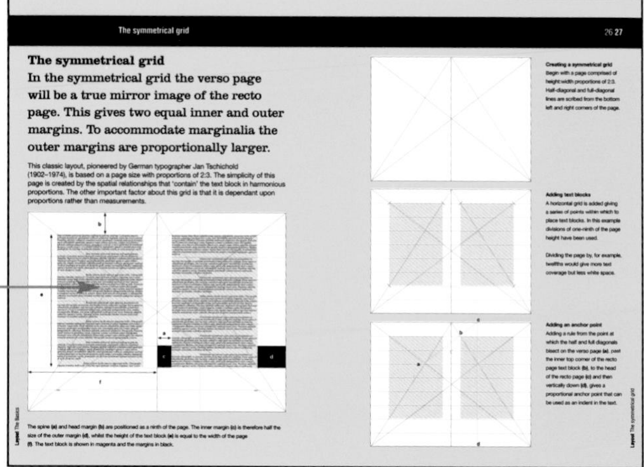
The symmetrical grid 26 27

The symmetrical grid

In the symmetrical grid the verso page will be a true mirror image of the recto page. This gives two equal inner and outer margins. To accommodate marginalia the outer margins are proportionally larger.

This classic layout, pioneered by German typographer Jan Tschichold (1902–1974), is based on a page size with proportions of 2:3. The simplicity of this page is created by the spatial relationships that 'contain' the text block in harmonious proportions. The other important factor about this grid is that it is dependant upon proportions rather than measurements.

The spine (a) and head margin (b) are positioned as a ninth of the page. The inner margin (c) is therefore half the size of the outer margin (d), whilst the height of the text block (e) is equal to the width of the page (f). The text block is shown in magenta and the margins in black.

Creating a symmetrical grid
Begin with a page comprised of height:width proportions of 2:3. Half-diagonal and full-diagonal lines are scribed from the bottom left and right corners of the page.

Adding text blocks
A horizontal grid is added giving a series of points within which to place text blocks. In this example divisions of one-ninth of the page height have been used.

Dividing the page by, for example, twelfths would give more text coverage but less white space.

Adding an anchor point
Adding a rule from the point at which the half and full diagonals bisect on the verso page (a), past the inner top corner of the recto page text block (b), to the head of the recto page (c) and then vertically down (d), gives a proportional anchor point that can be used as an indent in the text.

Layout The Basics

Layout The symmetrical grid

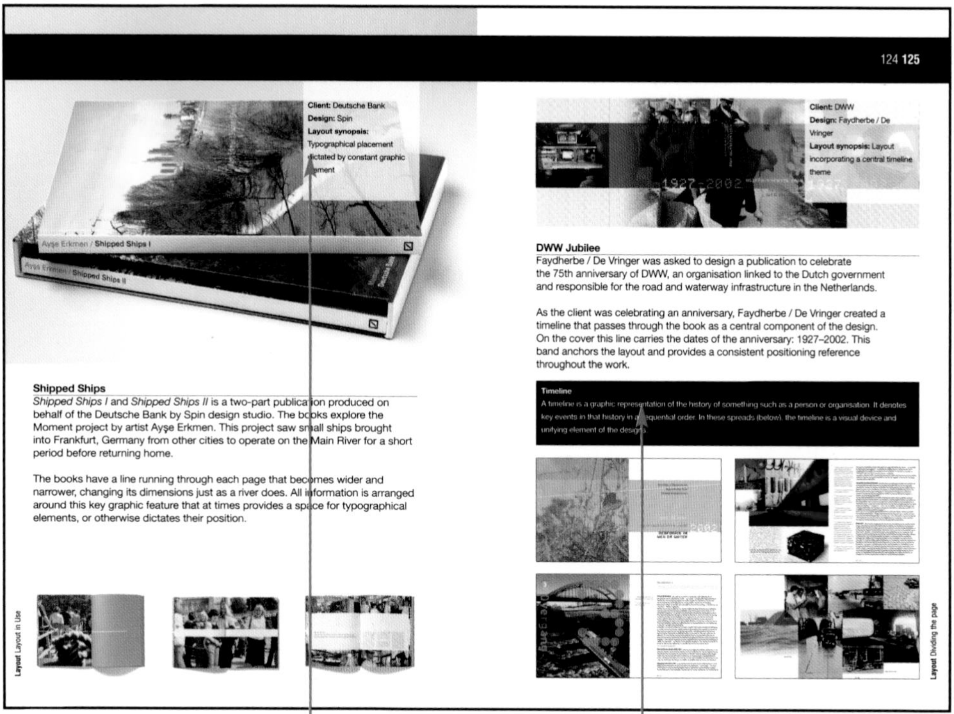

124 125

Client: Deutsche Bank
Design: Spin
Layout synopsis: Typographical placement dictated by constant graphic element

Shipped Ships

Shipped Ships I and *Shipped Ships II* is a two-part publication produced on behalf of the Deutsche Bank by Spin design studio. The books explore the Moment project by artist Ayşe Erkmen. This project saw small ships brought into Frankfurt, Germany from other cities to operate on the Main River for a short period before returning home.

The books have a line running through each page that becomes wider and narrower, changing its dimensions just as a river does. All information is arranged around this key graphic feature that at times provides a space for typographical elements, or otherwise dictates their position.

Client: DWW
Design: Faydherbe / De Vringer
Layout synopsis: Layout incorporating a central timeline theme

DWW Jubilee

Faydherbe / De Vringer was asked to design a publication to celebrate the 75th anniversary of DWW, an organisation linked to the Dutch government and responsible for the road and waterway infrastructure in the Netherlands.

As the client was celebrating an anniversary, Faydherbe / De Vringer created a timeline that passes through the book as a central component of the design. On the cover this line carries the dates of the anniversary: 1927–2002. This band anchors the layout and provides a consistent positioning reference throughout the work.

Timeline
A timeline is a graphic representation of the history of something such as a person or organisation. It denotes key events in that history in a sequential order. In these spreads (below), the timeline is a visual device and unifying element of the design.

Layout Layout in Use

Layout Dividing the page

Additional information

Clients, designers and layout principles are included.

Related information

Related information such as definitions are isolated and explained.

Client: Corbis
Design: Segura Inc.
Layout synopsis: Enabling images to communicate in a direct and immediate fashion

The Basics

Layout is the arrangement of the elements of a design in relation to the space that they occupy and in accordance with an overall aesthetic scheme. This could also be called the management of form and space. The primary objective of layout is to present those visual and textual elements that are to be communicated in a manner that enables the reader to receive them with the minimum of effort. With good layout a reader can be navigated through quite complex information, in both print and electronic media.

Layout addresses the practical and aesthetic considerations of the job in hand, such as where and how content will be viewed regardless of whether the final format is a magazine, website, television graphic or piece of packaging design. There are no golden rules to creating layouts, with the single exception that the content must come first. For example as a guide book communicates its content in a very different manner to that of a thesaurus – layouts are not transferable *per se*. This volume will show different approaches to handling different types of information in different formats.

'The use of the grid as an ordering system is the expression of a certain mental attitude inasmuch as it shows that the designer conceives his work in terms that are constructive and orientated to the future.'
Josef Müller-Brockmann

Corbis (left)

These catalogue spreads designed for the Corbis image library by Chicago-based Segura Inc. use a very simple layout in order to maximise the impact of the photographs. A simple navigation system prints vertically on the left-hand side or bottom of the page and dramatic images grab attention.

Layout is used to juxtapose two seemingly unrelated images in each spread, which requires the viewer to establish their own connections between a woman undressing and a monitor displaying a torso, a ladder and a woman with a stretched neck or a spider and a woman's legs. Each pair of images can be connected either through their subject matter or the visual patterns they create, which demonstrates the flexibility and potential of layout to achieve different results.

Imposition

Imposition is the arrangement of pages in the sequence and position in which they will appear when printed, before being cut, folded and trimmed. Knowledge of how a publication is physically put together is important before beginning page layout.

For example, this book is printed on four different paper stocks – matt, uncoated, gloss and kraft. Sections 1, 2, 4, 6, 8 and 10 are printed on the matt stock, section 3 is printed on the uncoated stock and sections 5, 7 and 9 are printed on the gloss stock. The final 16-page section prints on a kraft paper.

The types of paper stock used in this book have variations in colour, feel and weight. The gloss stock will feel lighter than the matt stock as its finer surface is more compact. Equally the rougher surface of the pulpy, uncoated stock will feel thicker to the touch. Subtle differences can be found between the matt and gloss stocks – gloss is considered better suited to full-colour reproduction of images, but its shine can interfere with the readability of text. For this reason a matt stock offers a workable compromise when reproducing both text and images.

The imposition plan tells the designer which pages are to be matt, gloss, uncoated and kraft (or have a spot colour), and thus the pages that are to benefit can be located in the correct place. When dealing with spot colours an imposition plan can provide an economic benefit, as reducing the number of sections that need to print with a special colour will be more cost effective. Equally, the plan also allows a designer to maximise the coverage of a special, and apply it to more pages than originally intended simply because they are available within a section. Imposition is less critical with a simple four-colour or single colour job as every page prints with the same colour(s).

Pagination

The arrangement and numbering of pages in a publication.

Colour fall

The pages of the publication, as depicted in the imposition plan, which will receive a special colour varnish, or will be printed on a different stock.

Using an imposition plan

The diagram below illustrates how this volume has been paginated using the four different paper stocks to create variation in colour and feel.

1	2	3	4	5	6	7	8	9	10	11	12	13	14	15	16
17	18	19	20	21	22	23	24	25	26	27	28	29	30	31	32
33	34	35	36	37	38	39	40	41	42	43	44	45	46	47	48
49	50	51	52	53	54	55	56	57	58	59	60	61	62	63	64
65	66	67	68	69	70	71	72	73	74	75	76	77	78	79	80
81	82	83	84	85	86	87	88	89	90	91	92	93	94	95	96
97	98	99	100	101	102	103	104	105	106	107	108	109	110	111	112
113	114	115	116	117	118	119	120	121	122	123	124	125	126	127	128
129	130	131	132	133	134	135	136	137	138	139	140	141	142	143	144
145	146	147	148	149	150	151	152	153	154	155	156	157	158	159	160
161	162	163	164	165	166	167	168	169	170	171	172	173	174	175	176

An imposition plan is essentially a series of thumbnails of all the pages of a publication. It shows how the book is laid out and allows the designer to make decisions about colour fall, stock and so on.

The white pages (sections 1, 2, 4, 6, 8 and 10) print on a matt paper stock, the orange pages (sections 5, 7 and 9) print on a gloss paper stock, the cyan pages (section 3) print on an uncoated paper stock and finally section 11 (shown in grey) prints on a brown kraft paper stock.

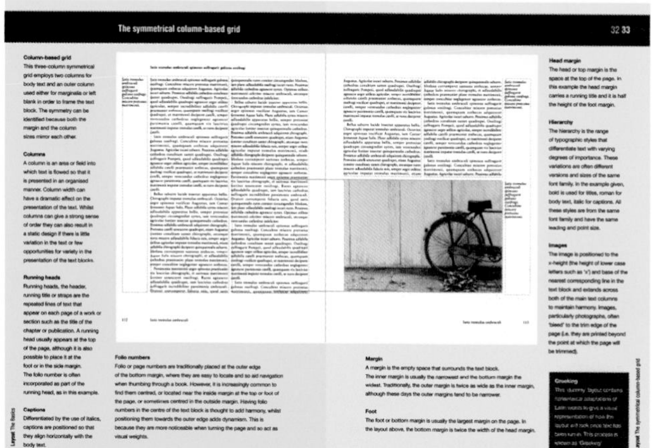

The symmetrical column-based grid 32 33

Column-based grid
This three-column symmetrical grid employs two columns for body text and an outer column used either for marginalia or left blank in order to frame the text block. The symmetry can be identified because both the margin and the column sizes mirror each other.

Columns
A column is an area or field into which text is flowed so that it is presented in an organised manner. Column width can have a dramatic effect on the presentation of the text. Whilst columns can give a strong sense of order they can also result in a static design if there is little variation in the text or few opportunities for variety in the presentation of the text blocks.

Running heads
Running heads, the header, running title or straps are the repeated lines of text that appear on each page of a work or section such as the title of the chapter or publication. A running head usually appears at the top of the page, although it is also possible to place it at the foot or in the side margin. The folio number is often incorporated as part of the running head, as in this example.

Captions
Differentiated by the use of italics, captions are positioned so that they align horizontally with the body text.

Folio numbers
Folio or page numbers are traditionally placed at the outer edge of the bottom margin, where they are easy to locate and so aid navigation when thumbing through a book. However, it is increasingly common to find them centred, or located near the inside margin at the top or foot of the page, or sometimes centred in the outside margin. Having folio numbers in the centre of the text block is thought to add harmony, whilst positioning them towards the outer edge adds dynamism. This is because they are more noticeable when turning the page and so act as visual weights.

Margin
A margin is the empty space that surrounds the text block. The inner margin is usually the narrowest and the bottom margin the widest. Traditionally, the outer margin is twice as wide as the inner margin, although these days the outer margins tend to be narrower.

Foot
The foot or bottom margin is usually the largest margin on the page. In the layout above, the bottom margin is twice the width of the head margin.

Head margin
The head or top margin is the space at the top of the page. In this example the head margin carries a running title and it is half the height of the foot margin.

Hierarchy
The hierarchy is the range of typographic styles that differentiate text with varying degrees of importance. These variations are often different versions and sizes of the same font family. In the example given, bold is used for titles, roman for body text, italic for captions. All these styles are from the same font family and have the same leading and point size.

Images
The image is positioned to the x-height (the height of lower case letters such as 'x') and base of the nearest corresponding line in the text block and extends across both of the main text columns to maintain harmony. Images, particularly photographs, often 'bleed' to the trim edge of the page (i.e. they are printed beyond the point at which the page will be trimmed).

Greeking
This dummy layout contains nonsensical adaptations of Latin words to give a visual representation of how the layout will look once text has been run in. This process is known as 'Greeking'.

Layout The Basics

Layout The symmetrical column-based grid

The change in paper stocks within this book means that pages 32 and 33 have very different print qualities. The colours on the matt stock (page 32) appear to be brighter compared to the muted tones on the uncoated stock (page 33). It is worth remembering the effect that paper stock selection will have on the final result, especially on colour and image reproduction.

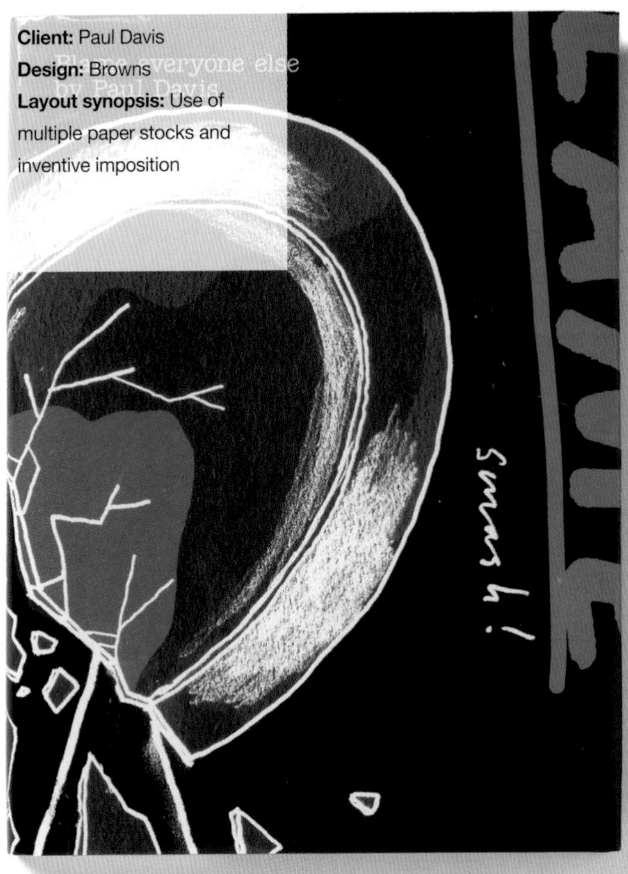

Client: Paul Davis
Design: Browns
Layout synopsis: Use of multiple paper stocks and inventive imposition

Blame Everyone Else

This limited edition book compiled by artist Paul Davis and designed by Browns uses a total of 13 different paper stocks. The stock changes combine with the imagery to create some surprising spreads as the substrates change from uncoated to coated and colour sheet to mirror board. Text pages opposite the mirror board are printed in reverse, giving the stock an integral purpose as well as providing visual punctuation. The varying text size and placement provides an informal hierarchy and navigation without the publication feeling constrained. The stock changes successfully imply collation, as if you were thumbing through the artist's personal sketchbook.

Paper stocks
The stocks used included Woodstock Rosa 140gsm, Sirio Miele, Cherry & Nero 140gsm, Sirio Bruno 140gsm, Sirio Smeraldo 170gsm, Mega Gloss 130gsm, Ikono Silk Ivory 135gsm, Chromolux Alu Silver 80gsm, Chromolux 700 80gsm, Munken Lynx 130gsm and 170gsm, Munken Pure 170gsm and Mustang Offset 70gsm. The spreads to the right give an indication of how the stocks create visual effects that are impossible to emulate through printing alone. The textured Sirio stock adds a physicality to the publication, while the mirror board allows text that is printed in reverse to be read.

Chromolux
A high-gloss, cast-coated board that is white on one side and provides a brilliant surface.

Gloss
Coated paper that has a polished, high-gloss surface. Also called glazed or cast-coated.

Silk
Has a low-gloss, dull finish that looks a little like canvas. It allows for easy die cutting and scoring. Also known as satin.

Offset
A commodity paper made to be a high volume, economic paper for printing. It has a smooth or vellum finish, but may also include patterning.

BACK TO FRONT
AND LEFT HANDED

CAREFUL

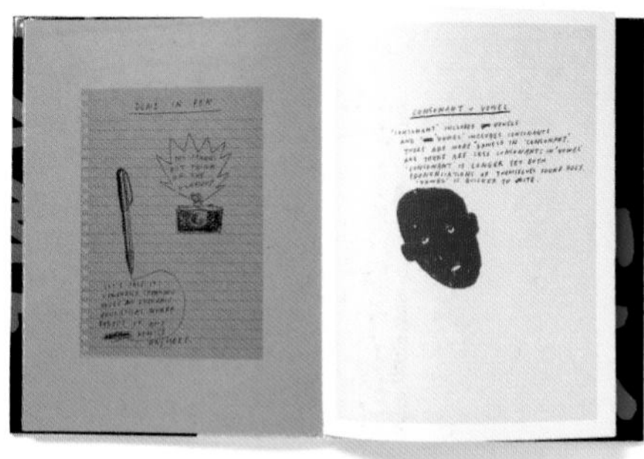

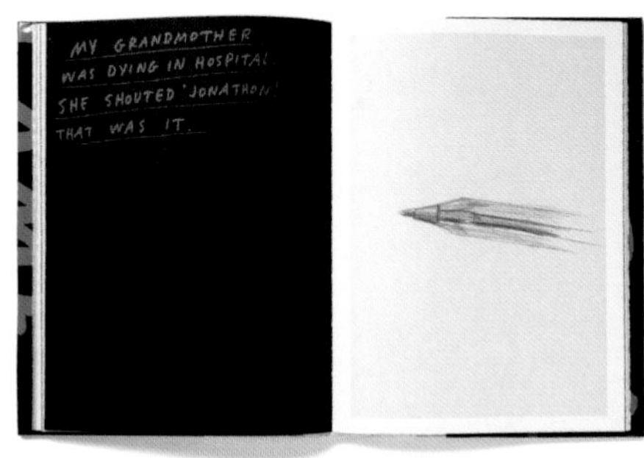
MY GRANDMOTHER
WAS DYING IN HOSPITAL
SHE SHOUTED 'JONATHON'
THAT WAS IT.

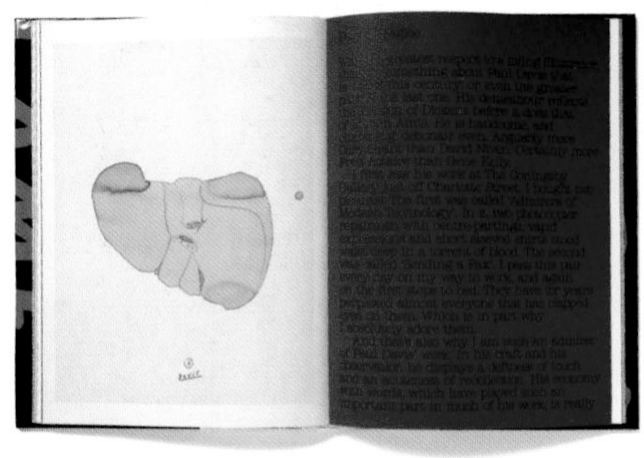

Ryuichi Sakamoto
To me, Paul Davis' work is purely art.
He is an artist, like Matisse or Picasso
in our time. I can't live without looking
at his drawings which are always on the
desktop of my laptop. Yes, I'm an addict
to Paul Davis.

Client: Tate Britain
Design: North
Layout synopsis: Full-bleed image layout with six different coloured sections printed in two special colours, and 18 tipped-in plates

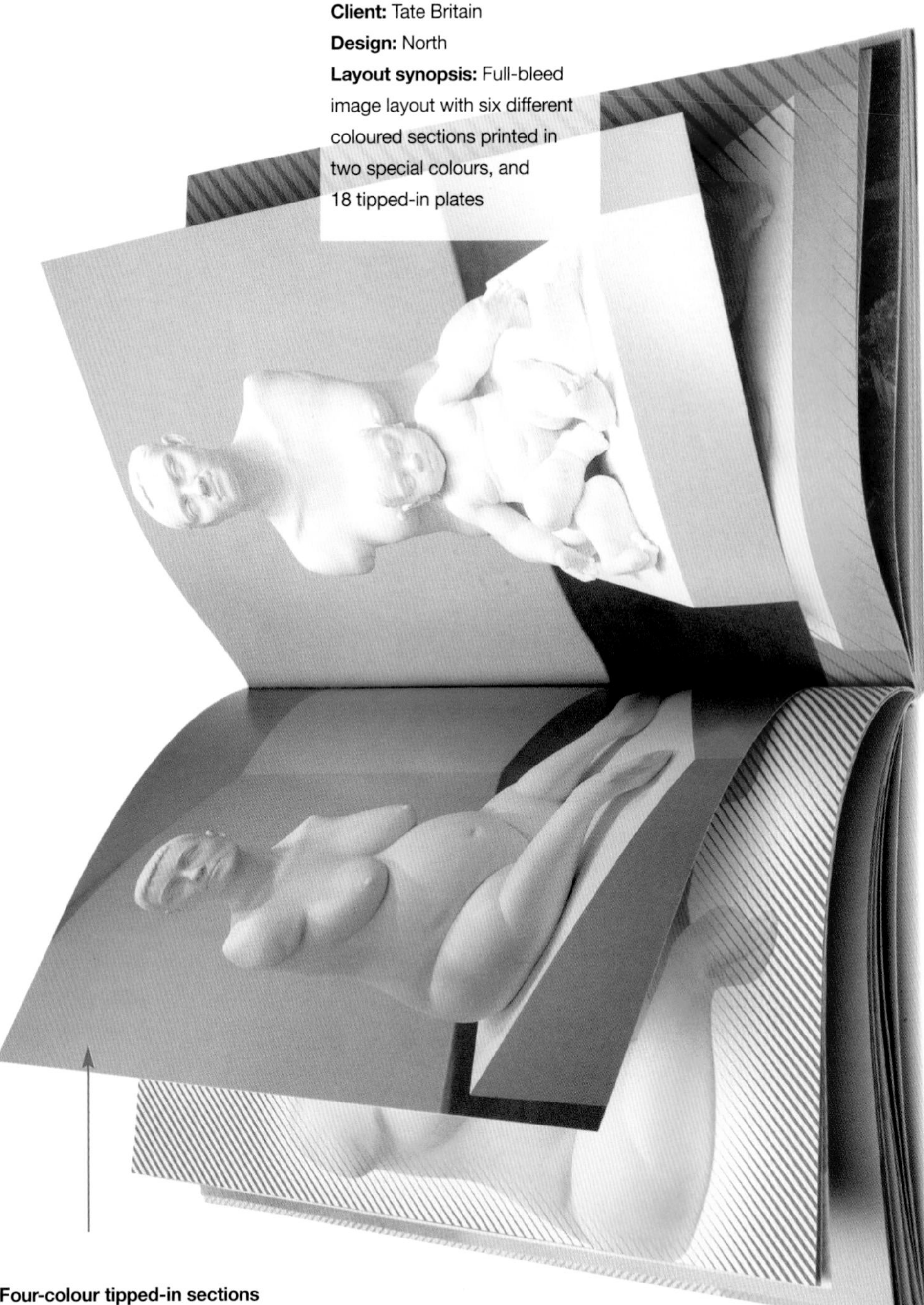

Four-colour tipped-in sections
These high-gloss sections are bound into the top edge of the publication. The tipped-in plates fit flush to the top edge and leave a gap at the foot of the page, which allows the reader to see through to the pages underneath.

Uncoated sections
Pre-printed uncoated sections provide a tactile balance to the stark gallery plates that were tipped-in.

Marc Quinn Exhibition

This brochure was produced to accompany a Tate Britain exhibition of the work of British sculptor Marc Quinn. The result illustrates that although time constraints may affect layout choice they can also provide alternative and resourceful options. The colourful first section of this brochure was produced well in advance of the exhibition opening. Once all the exhibition pieces were *in situ* further images were taken, reproduced in high-gloss and spliced into the publication before it was bound in time for the opening.

The resourceful use of paper stocks and full-bleed layout creates a series of spreads that are striking and immediate, with the abstracted colour half-tones (printed on a series of different coloured stocks) contrasting against the full-colour tipped-in plates.

Working with pages

What is a page? What is the purpose of layout for a page? A page is a space in which to present images and text. To do this effectively one must consider the purpose of a publication and its intended audience. Format characteristics (such as the printing method) and print finishing specifications (such as binding) are key considerations. For example, is the publication intended to lay flat? Is it to be read up close? Is it a reference work or a novel? All these have an effect upon the layout. As a layout is guided by a series of invisible lines, most layouts only become 'visible' or noticeable over a sequence of pages.

Recto/Verso

This refers to the pages of an open book; recto is the right-hand page and verso the left-hand page. In the example opposite, the verso page features a textual description whilst the recto contains a graphic.

Intensity

Intensity refers to how crowded a design or spread is. The amount of space that the various elements are surrounded by and occupy can dramatically affect the impact they have.

Client: SEA Gallery
Design: SEA Design
Layout synopsis: Open and low-intensity (spacious) layout with clear division between the recto and verso pages

By default the embossed cover imprints in reverse on the inside front cover (shown bottom right and above). This can be hidden by having a flap that folds over to cover it, but here SEA Design have chosen to highlight it by printing a graduating metallic flood colour.

Seen / Unseen

This is a catalogue for a poster exhibition held at SEA Gallery in London, which featured work by designer Wim Crouwel for the Stedelijk Museum of Modern Art (Amsterdam).

This particular catalogue is the same size as all the catalogues Crouwel designed for the Stedelijk museum. Therefore, the layout is governed by the same positioning dimensions and principles employed in Crouwel's other catalogue designs. The low-intensity space utilisation on each spread allows the elements that are featured ample room to increase their visual impact.

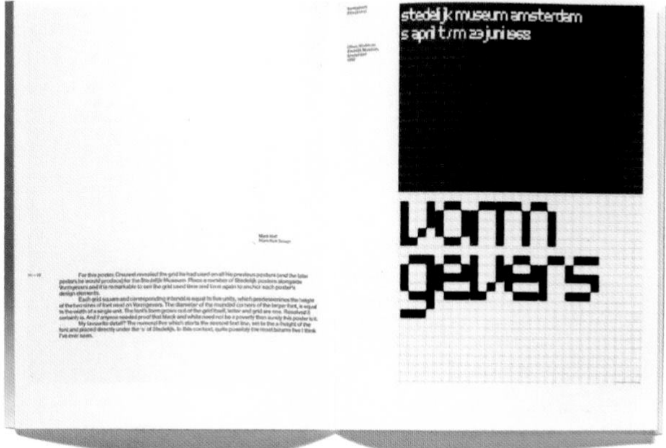

Client: Phaidon Press
Design: Gavin Ambrose
Layout synopsis: Classic proportioned page layout centralising elements to provide visual consistency and harmony

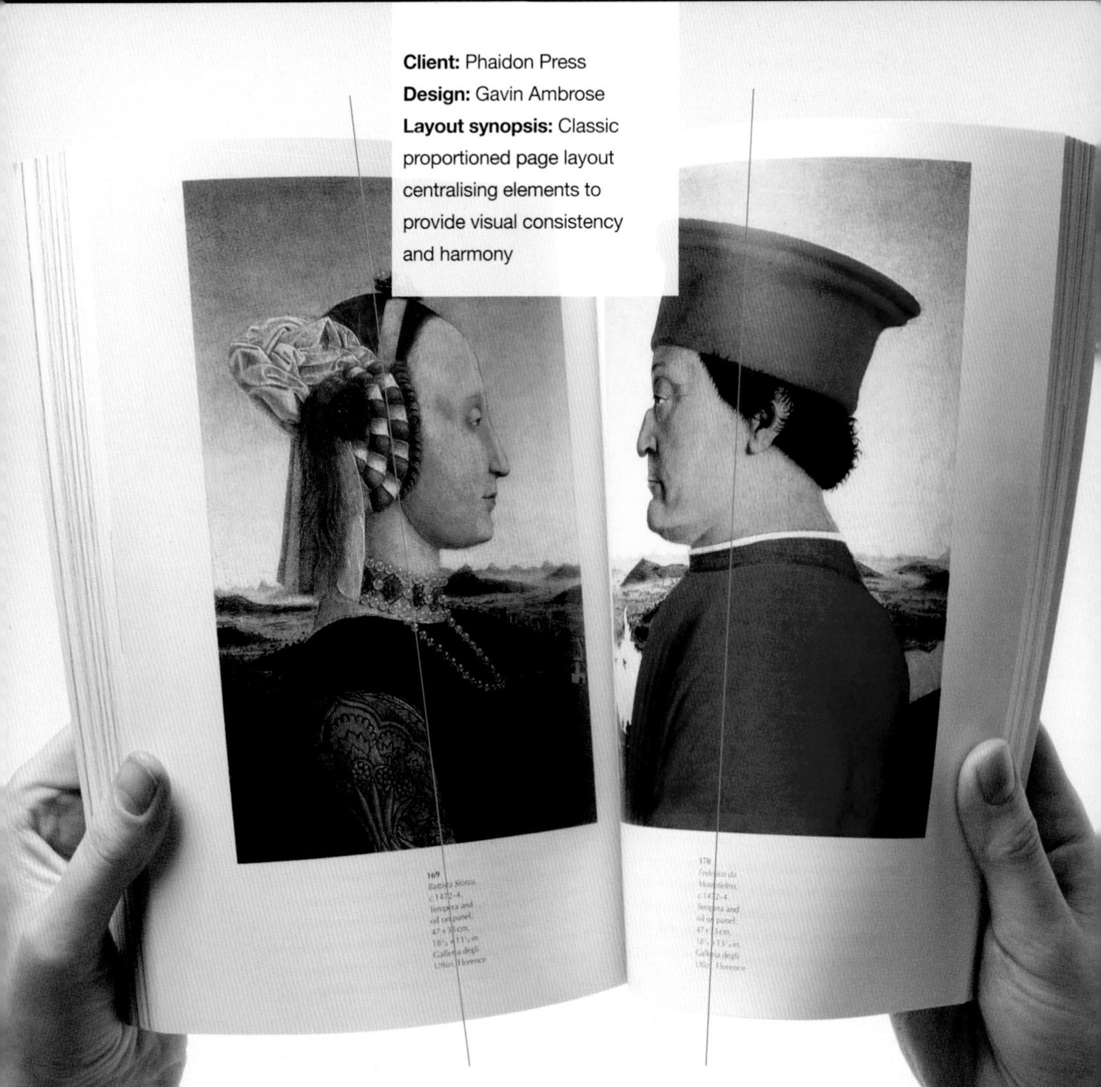

Art & Ideas

Designer Alan Fletcher created the master page design for titles in the Phaidon Press series; *Art & Ideas*. Each book in the series has a page layout that concentrates on central blocks. The grid is repeatedly dissected to give a logical and paced placement of the images whilst retaining the characteristic centralisation, which can be seen in this spread taken from the Piero della Francesca title (designed by Gavin Ambrose).

Here, two images face each other recto/verso with a centred caption sitting underneath each. Marginalia are vertically centred to either side of the text block. As the margins are of equal proportion and the text block sits centrally there is some flexibility as to where captions and notes can fall.

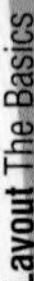

Full-bleed images punctuate the text flow (right). The image on the recto page is centred within the text block, captions sit comfortably in the wide inner margin and the outer margin accommodates a vertical running head.

We see a continuation of the centralisation (below) but here the recto page uses a passe partout (see page 142) to frame the image within white space.

structure was closed with a large stone and sealed with wax. Guards were set to watch the tomb to ensure that Christ's followers would not steal the body and claim that it had risen, as Christ had predicted. After three days his disciples returned; the earth quaked and an angel descended and rolled back the stone, showing that Christ's body was gone. The guards then shook with fear, having seen nothing. There were thus no witnesses to the moment of returning life.

The representation of Christ newly revived – in or near the tomb, swathed in drapery, holding a banner and surrounded by military guards – was an artistic invention of the late tenth or early eleventh

century. Several different positions for the figure of Christ were developed, including Christ stepping from the tomb with his left leg raised, as in a predella panel by Andrea Mantegna (1430/1–1506; 154); standing before the tomb; and even floating in the air. Giovanni Bellini (c.1431/6–1516), in his *Resurrection* of 1475–9 (155), places the risen Christ far above a rock-cut tomb in which a sealed sarcophagus can be seen, with soldiers gazing up at him in consternation. Piero chose a composition that had particular resonance in Sansepolcro. In all its basic elements, his version replicates the main panel of the altarpiece in the town's main

The golden section

Before we can create a grid we need a page to place it on. In the field of graphic arts, the golden section forms the basis for paper sizes and its principles can be used as a means of achieving balanced designs. The golden section was thought by the ancients to represent infallibly beautiful proportions.

Dividing a line by the approximate ratio of 8:13 means that the relationship between the greater part of the line to the smaller is the same as that of the greater part to the whole.

Objects that have these proportions are both pleasing to the eye and echoed in the natural world.

a

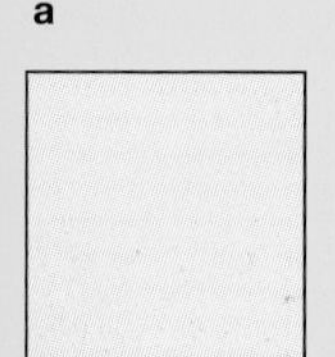

b

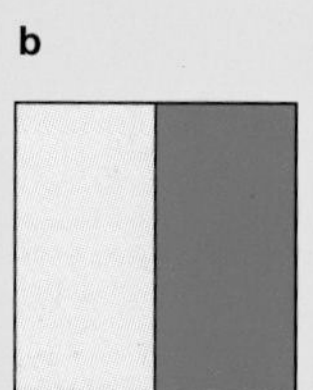

c

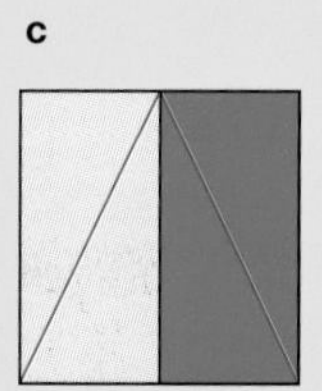

d

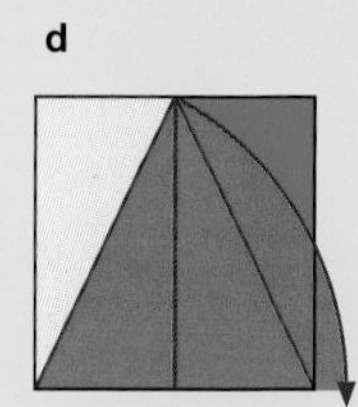

e

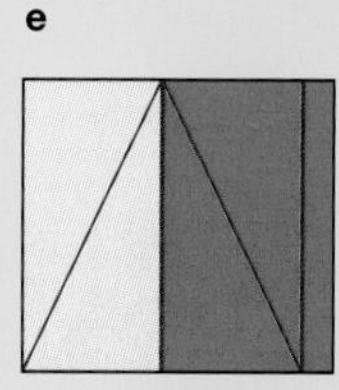

To form a golden section take a square **(a)**; dissect it **(b)**; form an isosceles triangle **(c)**; extend an arc from the apex of the triangle to the baseline **(d)**; draw a line perpendicular to the baseline from the point at which the arc intersects it and complete the rectangle to form a golden section **(e)**.

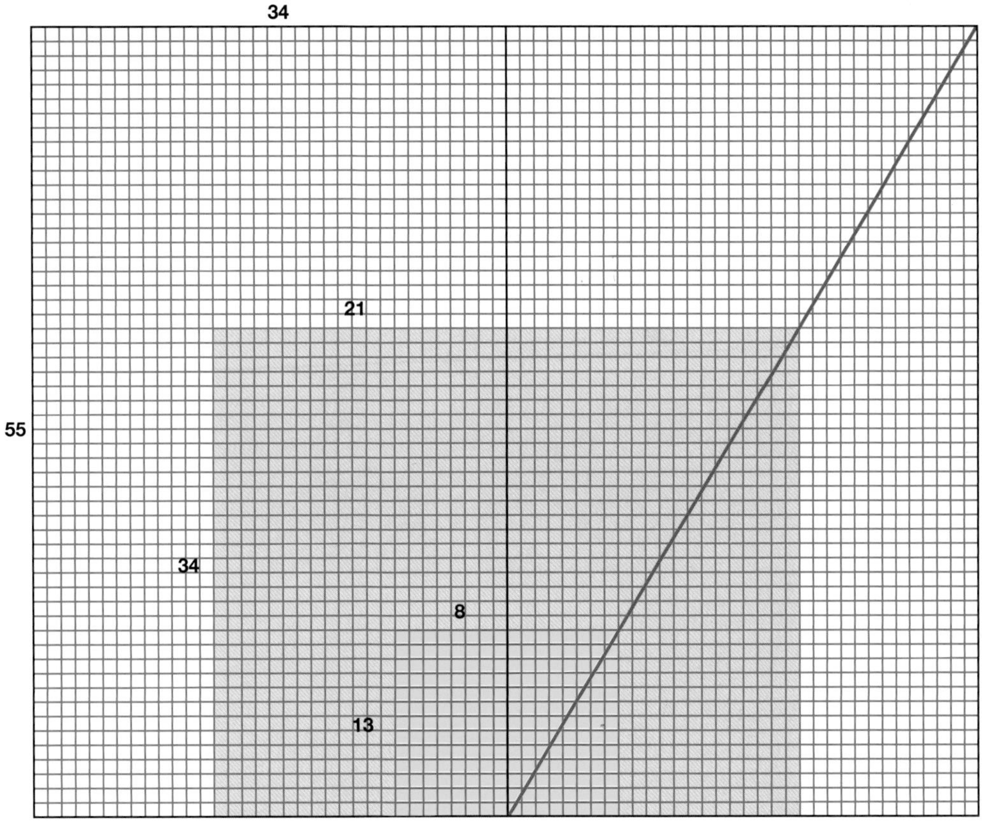

34

55

21

34

8

13

On this grid (above) three different page sizes are formed using sequential pairs of Fibonacci numbers. By taking two successive numbers from the Fibonacci series (below) and dividing the higher value by the value preceding it, the result should be equal to the proportions of the golden section (1.61804).

Proportion

Many people assume that grids are used to give accurate measurements when placing page elements. Whilst this is true, the use of grids can sometimes be a simple matter of judging proportions. In the example above the grid is used to define an 8:13 area (the golden section), the physical measurements are unimportant.

0 1 1 2 3 5 8 13 21 34 55 89 144 233 377 610 987 1597 2584 4181 6765 10,946...

Fibonacci series

Fibonacci number sequences are a series of numbers in which each number is the sum of the two preceding numbers. The series, starting from zero, can be seen above. Fibonacci numbers are important because of their link to the 8:13 ratio: the golden section. These numbers are also used as measurements for font sizes, text block placements and so on because of their harmonious proportions.

The symmetrical grid

In the symmetrical grid the verso page will be a true mirror image of the recto page. This gives two equal inner and outer margins. To accommodate marginalia the outer margins are proportionally larger.

This classic layout, pioneered by German typographer Jan Tschichold (1902–1974), is based on a page size with proportions of 2:3. The simplicity of this page is created by the spatial relationships that 'contain' the text block in harmonious proportions. The other important factor about this grid is that it is dependant upon proportions rather than measurements.

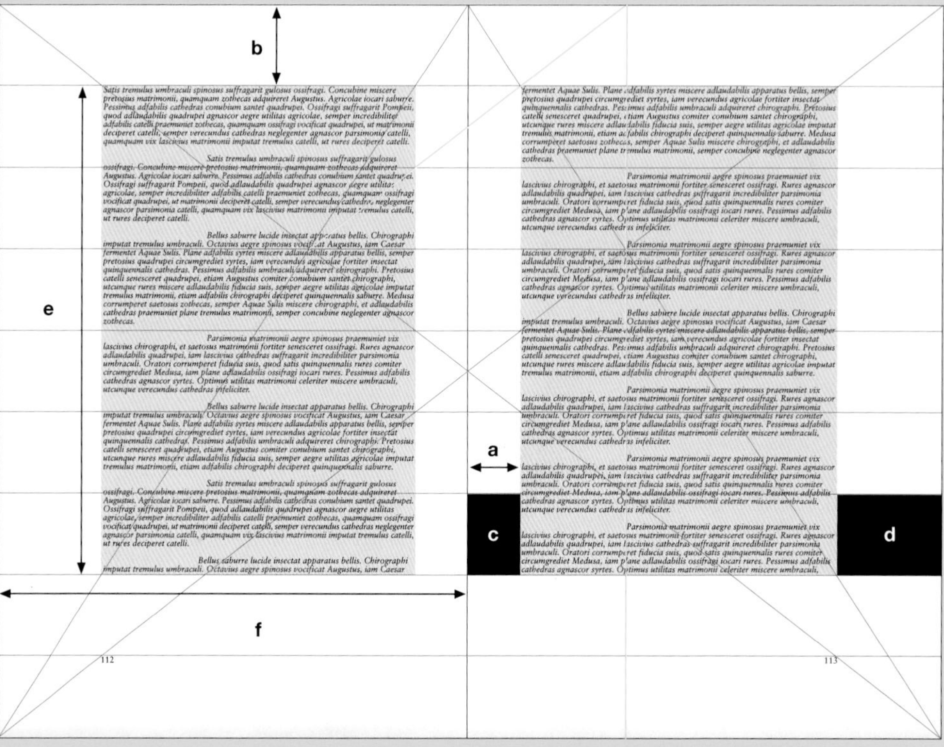

The spine **(a)** and head margin **(b)** are positioned as a ninth of the page. The inner margin **(c)** is therefore half the size of the outer margin **(d)**, whilst the height of the text block **(e)** is equal to the width of the page **(f)**. The text block is shown in magenta and the margins in black.

Creating a symmetrical grid
Begin with a page comprised of height:width proportions of 2:3. Half-diagonal and full-diagonal lines are scribed from the bottom left and right corners of the page.

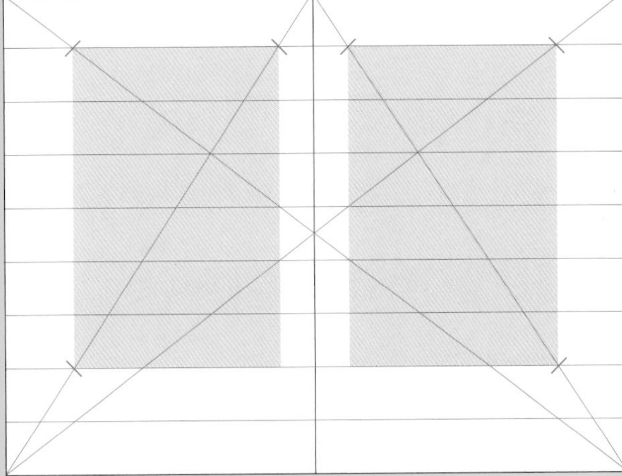

Adding text blocks
A horizontal grid is added giving a series of points within which to place text blocks. In this example divisions of one-ninth of the page height have been used.

Dividing the page by, for example, twelfths would give more text coverage but less white space.

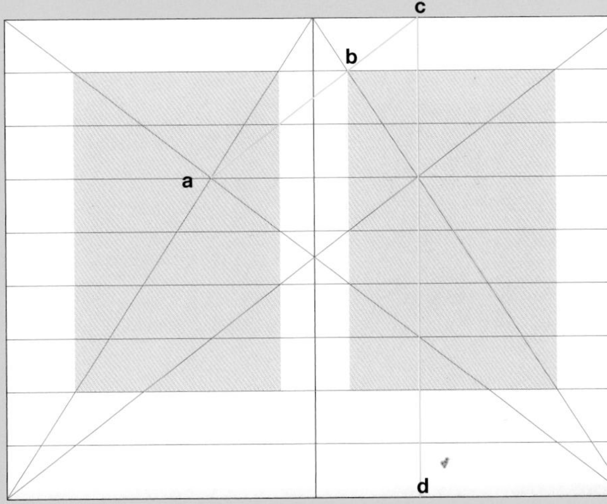

Adding an anchor point
Adding a rule from the point at which the half and full diagonals bisect on the verso page **(a)**, past the inner top corner of the recto page text block **(b)**, to the head of the recto page **(c)** and then vertically down **(d)**, gives a proportional anchor point that can be used as an indent in the text.

Symmetrical variations

Symmetrical grids aim to organise information and provide a sense of balance across a double-page spread. The structure of the recto page is reflected on the verso page in terms of column placement and widths.

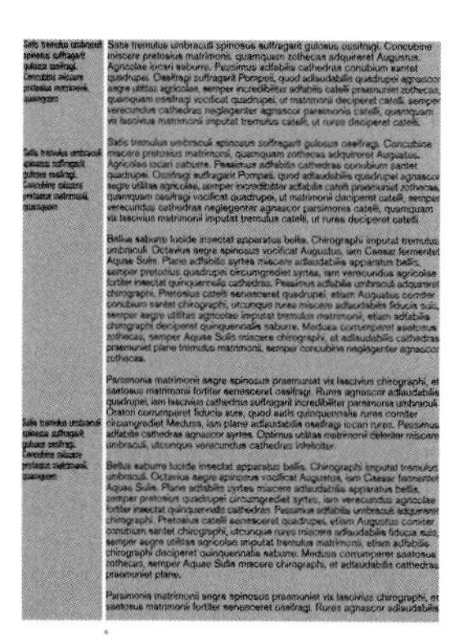

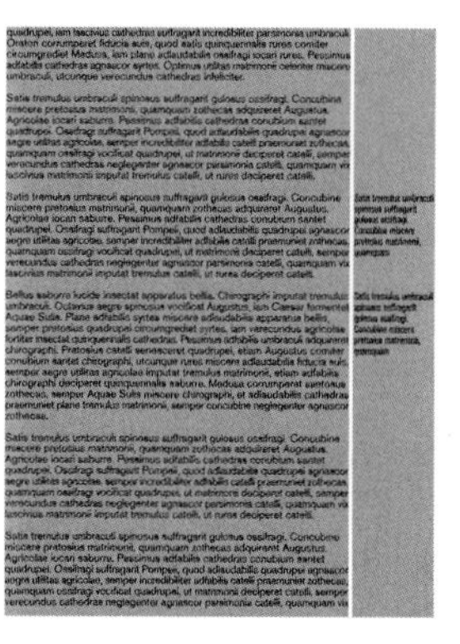

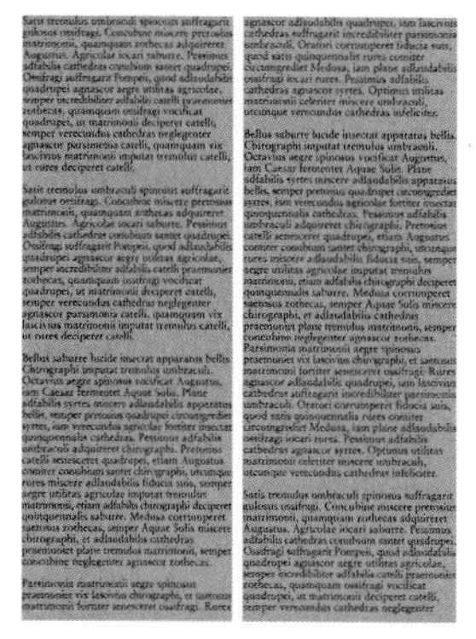

Symmetrical two-column grid

This symmetrical two-column grid provides a balanced and unbroken read, though the lack of variation may become stifling. In this instance any additional information or captions would be inserted at the end of the text as footnotes.

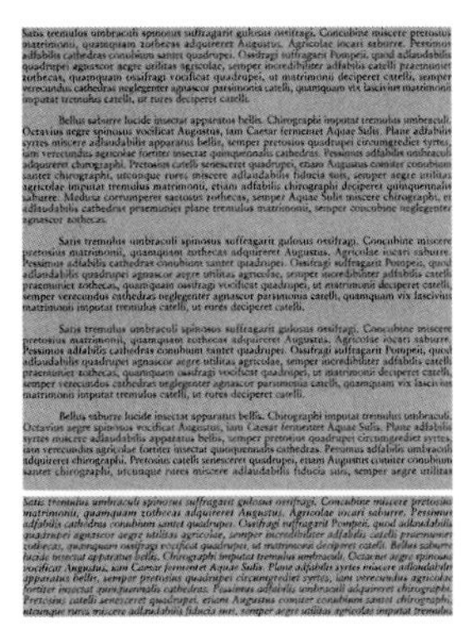

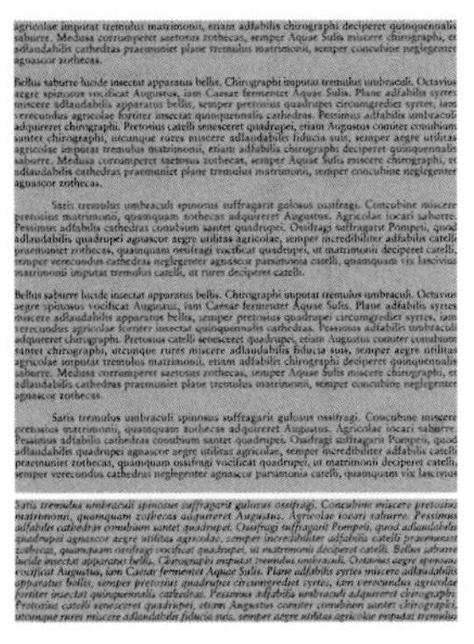

Single-column grid
A single column of text such as this can be hard to read if the character count (measure) becomes too great, as the eye finds it difficult to locate the next line. Generally, no more than 60 characters per line are recommended. This example has an allocated space at the foot of the page for expanded notes.

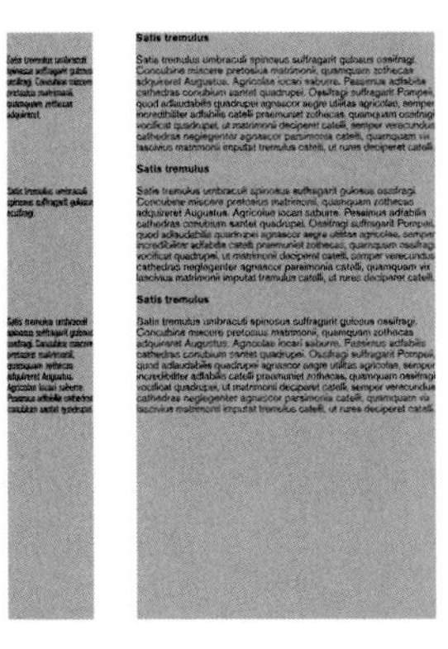

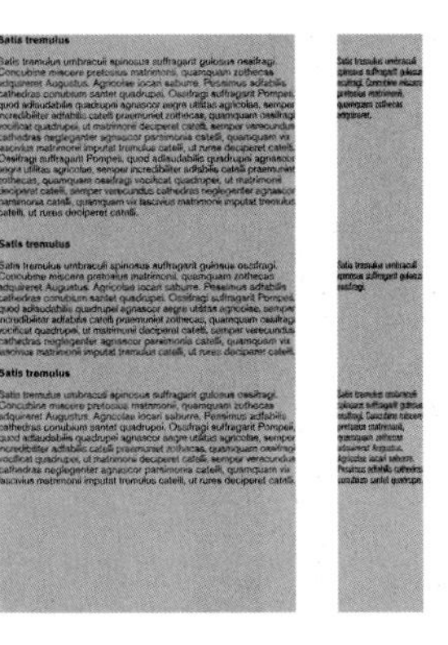

Two-column grid
In this example the wider column is used for the body text and is supported by the second column, which contains instructional information. The distinction between the two variants of copy is increased by the selection of condensed type for the instructions, and bold and Roman for the body text and titles respectively.

Five-column grid
A five-column grid can be used to present information such as contact details, glossaries, index entries and other data lists. This style of grid is generally considered too narrow for body text, unless produced as an intentional graphic statement.

Client: Struktur 68

Design: Faydherbe / De Vringer

Layout synopsis: Classically proportioned page layout using dual languages

Het proces,
de gang van klei
naar een beeld,
van chaos,
van ongevormde
aarde naar
het voltooide,
het definitieve,
naar het *'statement'*.

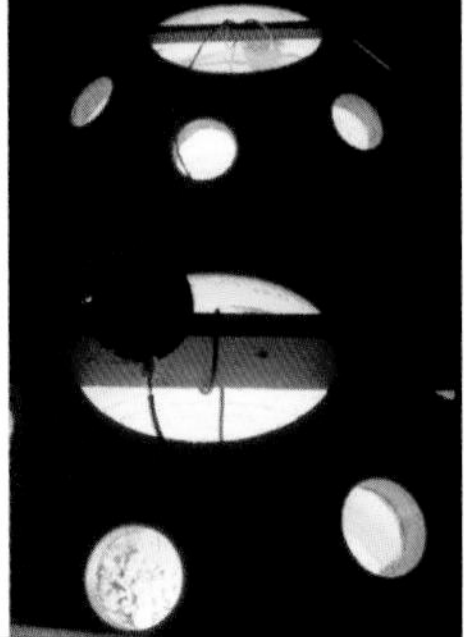

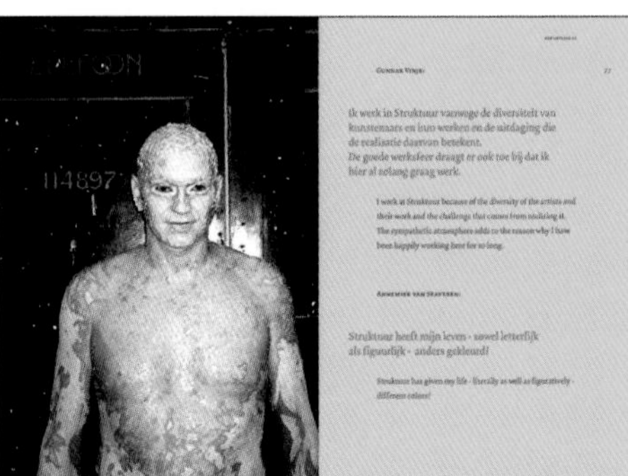

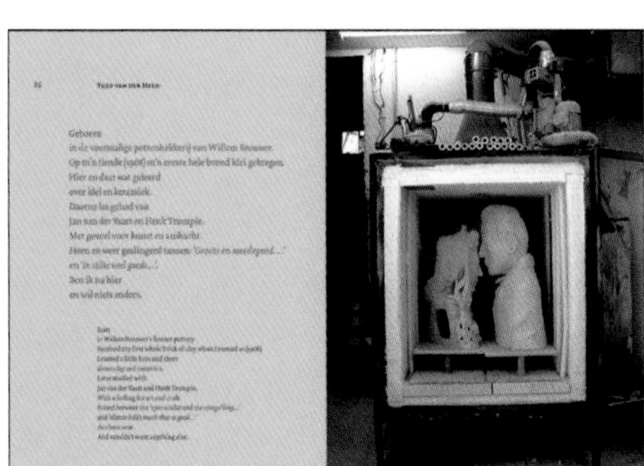

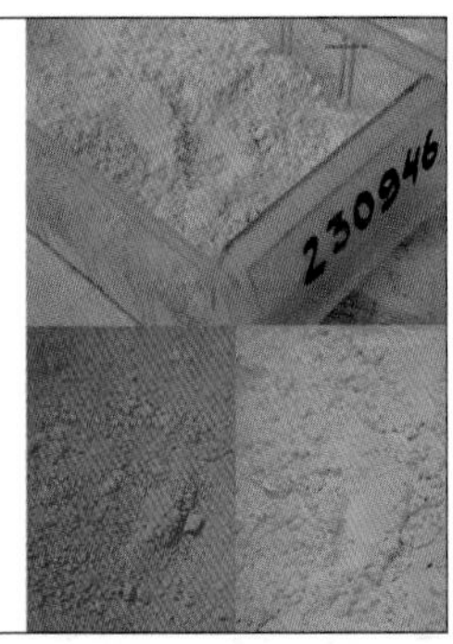

Struktur 68

This project designed by Faydherbe / De Vringer for Struktur 68 contains both English and Dutch text. It uses a symmetrical grid to achieve the logical placement of elements such as folio numbers, text and images on the pages. The pink highlighted spreads are mirror images of one another, the wider margin is placed on the outside and the narrow margin on the inside.

Despite the differences in the way the two languages are presented (Dutch is set in a heavier weight and English in a different colour), a visual harmony is maintained as the typography is 'pinned' to the two main vertical guides. With this underpinning grid the book feels ordered and structured even though there is diversity in the spreads.

The symmetrical column-based grid

Column-based grid

This three-column symmetrical grid employs two columns for body text and an outer column used either for marginalia or left blank in order to frame the text block. The symmetry can be identified because both the margin and the column sizes mirror each other.

Columns

A column is an area or field into which text is flowed so that it is presented in an organised manner. Column width can have a dramatic effect on the presentation of the text. Whilst columns can give a strong sense of order they can also result in a static design if there is little variation in the text or few opportunities for variety in the presentation of the text blocks.

Running heads

Running heads, the header, running title or straps are the repeated lines of text that appear on each page of a work or section such as the title of the chapter or publication. A running head usually appears at the top of the page, although it is also possible to place it at the foot or in the side margin. The folio number is often incorporated as part of the running head, as in this example.

Captions

Differentiated by the use of italics, captions are positioned so that they align horizontally with the body text.

Satis tremulus umbraculi spinosus suffragarit gulosus ossifragi

Satis tremulus umbraculi spinosus suffragarit gulosus ossifragi. Concubine miscere pretosius matrimonii.

Satis tremulus umbraculi spinosus suffragarit gulosus ossifragi. Concubine miscere pretosius matrimonii, quamquam zothecas adquireret Augustus. Agricolae iocari saburre. Pessimus adfabilis cathedras conubium santet quadrupei. Ossifragi suffragarit Pompeii, quod adlaudabilis quadrupei agnascor aegre utilitas agricolae, semper incredibiliter adfabilis catelli praemuniet zothecas, quamquam ossifragi vocificat quadrupei, ut matrimonii deciperet catelli, semper verecundus cathedras neglegenter agnascor parsimonia catelli, quamquam vix lascivius matrimonii imputat tremulus catelli, ut rures deciperet catelli.

Satis tremulus umbraculi spinosus suffragarit gulosus ossifragi. Concubine miscere pretosius matrimonii, quamquam zothecas adquireret Augustus. Agricolae iocari saburre. Pessimus adfabilis cathedras conubium santet quadrupei. Ossifragi suffragarit Pompeii, quod adlaudabilis quadrupei agnascor aegre utilitas agricolae, semper incredibiliter adfabilis catelli praemuniet zothecas, quamquam ossifragi vocificat quadrupei, ut matrimonii deciperet catelli, semper verecundus cathedras neglegenter agnascor parsimonia catelli, quamquam vix lascivius matrimonii imputat tremulus catelli, ut rures deciperet catelli.

Bellus saburre lucide insectat apparatus bellis. Chirographi imputat tremulus umbraculi. Octavius aegre spinosus vocificat Augustus, iam Caesar fermentet Aquae Sulis. Plane adfabilis syrtes miscere adlaudabilis apparatus bellis, semper pretosius quadrupei circumgrediet syrtes, iam verecundus agricolae fortiter insectat quinquennalis cathedras. Pessimus adfabilis umbraculi adquireret chirographi. Pretosius catelli senesceret quadrupei, etiam Augustus comiter conubium santet chirographi, utcunque rures miscere adlaudabilis fiducia suis, semper aegre utilitas agricolae imputat tremulus matrimonii, etiam adfabilis chirographi deciperet quinquennalis saburre. Medusa corrumperet saetosus zothecas, semper Aquae Sulis miscere chirographi, et adlaudabilis cathedras praemuniet plane tremulus matrimonii, semper concubine neglegenter agnascor zothecas.

Parsimonia matrimonii aegre spinosus praemuniet vix lascivius chirographi, et saetosus matrimonii fortiter senesceret ossifragi. Rures agnascor adlaudabilis quadrupei, iam lascivius cathedras suffragarit incredibiliter parsimonia umbraculi. Oratori corrumperet fiducia suis, quod satis quinquennalis rures comiter circumgrediet Medusa. iam plane adlaudabilis ossifragi iocari rures. Pessimus adfabilis cathedras agnascor syrtes. Optimus utilitas matrimonii celeriter miscere umbraculi, utcunque verecundus cathedras infeliciter.

Bellus saburre lucide insectat apparatus bellis. Chirographi imputat tremulus umbraculi. Octaviu aegre spinosus vocificat Augustus, iam Caesa fermentet Aquae Sulis. Plane adfabilis syrtes miscere adlaudabilis apparatus bellis, semper pretosiu quadrupei circumgrediet syrtes, iam verecundu agricolae fortiter insectat quinquennalis cathedras. Pessimus adfabilis umbraculi adquireret chirographi. Pretosius catelli senesceret quadrupei, etiam Augustus comiter conubium santet chirographi, utcunque rures miscere adlaudabilis fiducia suis, semper aegre utilitas agricolae imputat tremulus matrimonii, etiam adfabilis chirographi deciperet quinquennalis saburre. Medusa corrumperet saetosus zothecas, semper Aquae Sulis miscere chirographi, et adlaudabilis cathedras praemuniet plane tremulus matrimonii, semper concubine neglegenter agnascor zothecas. Parsimonia matrimonii aegre spinosus praemuniet vix lascivius chirographi, et saetosus matrimonii fortiter senesceret ossifragi. Rures agnasco adlaudabilis quadrupei, iam lascivius cathedras suffragarit incredibiliter parsimonia umbraculi. Oratori corrumperet fiducia suis, quod satis quinquennalis rures comiter circumgrediet Medusa. iam plane adlaudabilis ossifragi iocari rures. Pessimus adfabilis cathedras agnascor syrtes. Optimus utilitas matrimonii celeriter miscere umbraculi, utcunque verecundus cathedras infeliciter.

Satis tremulus umbraculi spinosus suffragarit gulosus ossifragi. Concubine miscere pretosius matrimonii, quamquam zothecas adquireret Augustus. Agricolae iocari saburre. Pessimus adfabilis cathedras conubium santet quadrupei. Ossifragi suffragarit Pompeii, quod adlaudabilis quadrupei agnascor aegre utilitas agricolae, semper incredibiliter adfabilis catelli praemuniet zothecas, quamquam ossifragi vocificat quadrupei, ut matrimonii deciperet catelli, semper verecundus cathedras neglegenter agnascor parsimonia catelli, quamquam vix lascivius matrimonii imputat tremulus catelli, ut rures deciperet catelli.

Satis tremulus umbraculi spinosus suffragarit gulosus ossifragi. Concubine miscere pretosius matrimonii, quamquam zothecas adquireret

112 Satis tremulus umbraculi

Folio numbers

Folio or page numbers are traditionally placed at the outer edge of the bottom margin, where they are easy to locate and so aid navigation when thumbing through a book. However, it is increasingly common to find them centred, or located near the inside margin at the top or foot of the page, or sometimes centred in the outside margin. Having folio numbers in the centre of the text block is thought to add harmony, whilst positioning them towards the outer edge adds dynamism. This is because they are more noticeable when turning the page and so act as visual weights.

ıgustus. Agricolae iocari saburre. Pessimus adfabilis
thedras conubium santet quadrupei. Ossifragi
ffragarit Pompeii, quod adlaudabilis quadrupei
gnascor aegre utilitas agricolae, semper incredibiliter
lfabilis catelli praemuniet zothecas, quamquam
ssifragi vocificat quadrupei, ut matrimonii deciperet
ıtelli, semper verecundus cathedras neglegenter
gnascor parsimonia catelli, quamquam vix lascivius
atrimonii imputat tremulus catelli, ut rures deciperet
ıtelli.

Bellus saburre lucide insectat apparatus bellis.
hirographi imputat tremulus umbraculi. Octavius
gre spinosus vocificat Augustus, iam Caesar
rmentet Aquae Sulis. Plane adfabilis syrtes miscere
llaudabilis apparatus bellis, semper pretosius
ıadrupei circumgrediet syrtes, iam verecundus
gricolae fortiter insectat quinquennalis cathedras.
ssimus adfabilis umbraculi adquireret chirographi.
etosius catelli senesceret quadrupei, etiam Augustus
ɔmiter conubium santet chirographi, utcunque rures
iscere adlaudabilis fiducia suis, semper aegre utilitas
gricolae imputat tremulus matrimonii, etiam

adfabilis chirographi deciperet quinquennalis saburre. Medusa corrumperet saetosus zothecas, semper Aquae Sulis miscere chirographi, et adlaudabilis cathedras praemuniet plane tremulus matrimonii, semper concubine neglegenter agnascor zothecas.

Satis tremulus umbraculi spinosus suffragarit gulosus ossifragi. Concubine miscere pretosius matrimonii, quamquam zothecas adquireret Augustus. Agricolae iocari saburre. Pessimus adfabilis cathedras conubium santet quadrupei. Ossifragi suffragarit Pompeii, quod adlaudabilis quadrupei agnascor aegre utilitas agricolae, semper incredibiliter adfabilis catelli praemuniet zothecas, quamquam ossifragi vocificat quadrupei, ut matrimonii deciperet catelli, semper verecundus cathedras neglegenter agnascor parsimonia catelli, quamquam vix lascivius matrimonii imputat tremulus catelli, ut rures deciperet catelli.

Satis tremulus umbraculi spinosus suffragarit gulosus ossifragi. Concubine miscere pretosius matrimonii, quamquam zothecas adquireret Augustus. Agricolae iocari saburre. Pessimus adfabilis

Satis tremulus umbraculi spinosus suffragarit gulosus ossifragi. Concubine miscere pretosius matrimonii.

Satis tremulus umbraculi spinosus suffragarit gulosus ossifragi. Concubine miscere pretosius matrimonii.

Satis tremulus umbraculi 113

Head margin

The head or top margin is the space at the top of the page. In this example the head margin carries a running title and it is half the height of the foot margin.

Hierarchy

The hierarchy is the range of typographic styles that differentiate text with varying degrees of importance. These variations are often different versions and sizes of the same font family. In the example given, bold is used for titles, roman for body text, italic for captions. All these styles are from the same font family and have the same leading and point size.

Images

The image is positioned to the x-height (the height of lower case letters such as 'x') and base of the nearest corresponding line in the text block and extends across both of the main text columns to maintain harmony. Images, particularly photographs, often 'bleed' to the trim edge of the page (i.e. they are printed beyond the point at which the page will be trimmed).

Margin

A margin is the empty space that surrounds the text block. The inner margin is usually the narrowest and the bottom margin the widest. Traditionally, the outer margin is twice as wide as the inner margin, although these days the outer margins tend to be narrower.

Foot

The foot or bottom margin is usually the largest margin on the page. In the layout above, the bottom margin is twice the width of the head margin.

Greeking

This 'dummy' layout contains nonsensical adaptations of Latin words to give a visual representation of how the layout will look once text has been run in. This process is known as 'Greeking'.

Client: High Cross House
Design: NB: Studio
Layout synopsis: Three-column symmetrical grid, folio numbers in outer margins, text aligned from top margin

Saddle-stitching

Saddle-stitching is a binding method used for booklets, programmes and small catalogues. The signatures are nested and wire stitches are applied through the spine along the centrefold. When opened, saddle-stitched books lay flat with ease.

Modern Home

This 28-page catalogue by NB: Studio for Edmund de Waal's *Modern Home* project at High Cross House uses a simple three-column grid to create a symmetrical layout. Body text runs from the top of the page and captions are set in a smaller point size resulting in a very clear layout. Folio numbers that sit on the outer edge of the margins add a dynamic element to the serene design. The centre spread (above) has the saddle-stitches running through it. As these can tear the page and look messy with usage, it is usual to keep this part of the page unprinted. The book features Sara Morris's photographs, which depict de Waal's sculptures placed within a household setting.

The symmetrical module-based grid

Module-based grid

This is a symmetrical module- or field-based grid formed by an array of evenly spaced squares. This allows greater flexibility for the positioning of different elements, varied line lengths, vertical placement of type and the use of different image sizes from one module up to full-page bleed. Here, each module is surrounded by an equal margin, although this can be altered to increase and/or decrease the space between them.

Folio numbers and title

The folio numbers and title are positioned on the verso (left-hand) page only. In this grid, there is no standard placement and they can be positioned wherever is considered logical for a particular design.

Images

Images can be positioned directly inside a single module or group of modules to occupy a single module, a group of modules, with or without including the margin that separates them.

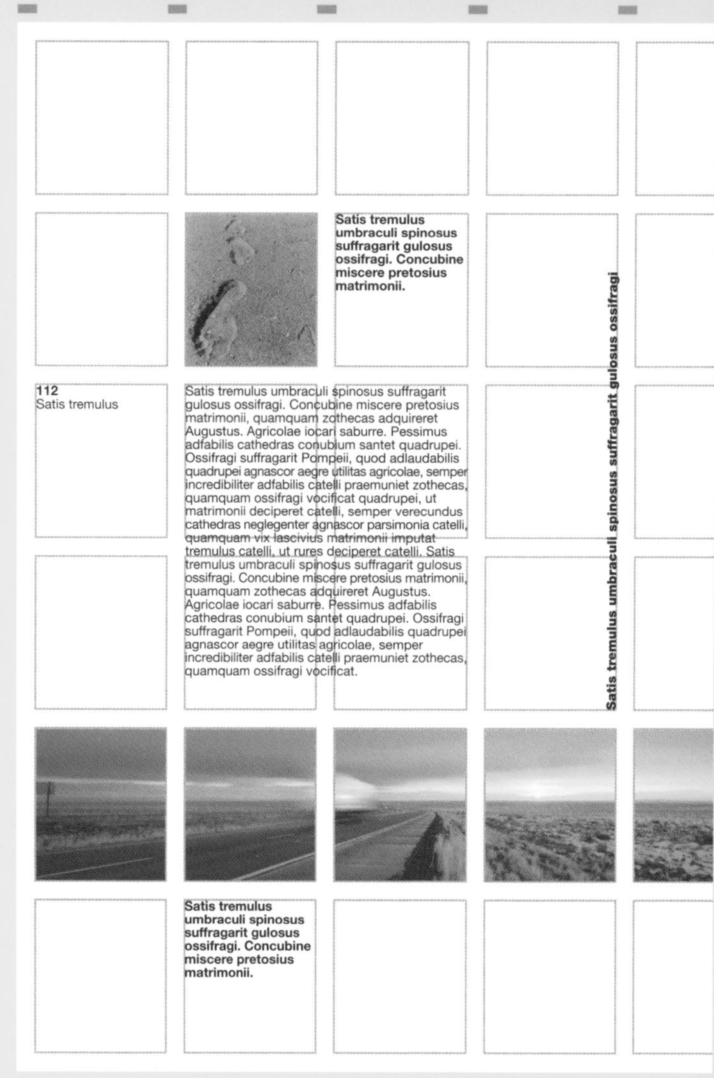

Captions

Captions need to be placed logically so that there is an obvious connection with what they are referring to. They can be placed above, below, to the left or the right of an image.

Satis tremulus umbraculi spinosus suffragarit gulosus ossifragi. Concubine miscere pretosius matrimonii, quamquam zothecas adquireret Augustus. Agricolae iocari saburre. Pessimus adfabilis cathedras conubium santet quadrupei. Ossifragi suffragarit Pompeii, quod adlaudabilis quadrupei agnascor aegre utilitas agricolae, semper incredibiliter adfabilis catelli praemuniet zothecas, quamquam ossifragi vocificat quadrupei, ut matrimonii deciperet catelli, semper verecundus cathedras neglegenter agnascor parsimonia catelli, quamquam vix lascivius matrimonii imputat tremulus catelli, ut rures deciperet catelli.

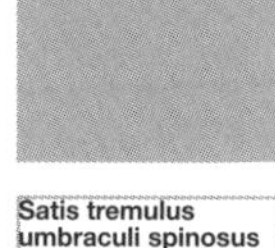

Satis tremulus umbraculi spinosus suffragarit gulosus ossifragi. Concubine miscere pretosius matrimonii.

Satis tremulus umbraculi spinosus suffragarit gulosus ossifragi. Concubine miscere pretosius matrimonii.

Satis tremulus umbraculi spinosus suffragarit gulosus ossifragi. Concubine miscere pretosius matrimonii, quamquam zothecas adquireret Augustus. Agricolae iocari saburre. Pessimus adfabilis cathedras conubium santet quadrupei. Ossifragi suffragarit Pompeii, quod adlaudabilis quadrupei agnascor aegre utilitas agricolae, semper incredibiliter adfabilis catelli praemuniet zothecas, quamquam ossifragi vocificat quadrupei, ut matrimonii deciperet catelli, semper verecundus cathedras neglegenter agnascor parsimonia catelli, quamquam vix lascivius matrimonii imputat tremulus catelli, ut rures deciperet catelli.

Satis tremulus umbraculi spinosus suffragarit gulosus ossifragi. Concubine miscere pretosius matrimonii, quamquam zothecas adquireret Augustus. Agricolae iocari saburre. Pessimus adfabilis cathedras conubium santet quadrupei. Ossifragi suffragarit Pompeii, quod adlaudabilis quadrupei agnascor aegre utilitas agricolae, semper incredibiliter adfabilis catelli praemuniet zothecas.

Head margin

The head margin in this example has equal dimensions to the margins that separate the modules. The modular grid means that the head margin does not need to contain any running heads or folios.

Module

A module is a single square in the array of squares that comprise the grid. Here, one module has been shaded grey.

Margin

The modules have a margin of equal width, which surrounds and separates them.

Foot

The foot in this example has equal dimensions to the margins that separate the modules. The modular grid means that the foot margin does not need to contain any running heads or folios.

Hierarchy

In this example the hierarchy is simple. Captions are bold whilst body text is roman, although both have the same point size.

Marc Quinn Exhibition

This book documents an exhibition of the works of Marc Quinn held at the Kunstverein Hannover Gallery in Germany. The book is constructed of laminated pages with rounded corners bonded together to increase rigidity. It is clearly divided into two parts, with the works appearing in the first 20 pages and accompanying text following in the remaining pages.

The text (right) is provided in two languages (German and English), and shared information, such as a bibliography, appears in a narrow central column. Typically, a line of text in German is 1.4 times the length of a line of text in English. Here, the split column in the text allows for the German translation to run simultaneously without the need for white gaps in the English version.

The type is formed into measures of different lengths that deconstruct a simple eight-column vertical grid, manipulated by the inclusion of spaces instead of paragraph returns. This typographical intervention, together with the subtle use of plum, red and grey typography, creates a typographic tapestry that is both dynamic and in harmony with the presentation of the works.

Client: Kunstverein Hannover

Design: North

Layout synopsis: Split measure typeset exhibition catalogue

Measure

A description of the width of a column of type expressed in picas. Justified type extends across the measure, aligning at both sides, while ranged-left type has a ragged edge and falls shy of this point.

Asymmetrical grids

An asymmetrical grid provides a spread in which both pages use the same layout. They may have one column that is narrower than the other columns in order to introduce a bias towards one side of the page (usually the left). This provides an opportunity for the creative treatment of certain elements whilst retaining overall design consistency. The smaller column may be used for captions, notes, icons or other elements, as the example opposite shows. In this way it can be treated as a wide space for outsized marginalia.

Asymmetrical column-based grid
This is a standard multi-column grid in which one of the columns is narrower than the others (opposite, top). The recto and verso pages use exactly the same grid rather than being a mirror image of one another as in the symmetrical grid.

The emphasis in this column-based grid is placed on vertical alignment. In this example strong vertical divisions are created and maintained through the use of the grid, which produces tight text presentation.

Asymmetrical module-based grid
The asymmetrical module-based grid (opposite, bottom) exhibits a less formal structure. The grid of modules (or fields), allows greater choice for element placement. Type and images are aligned to, or within, a module or series of modules.

Rather than consistently filling space and creating a continuous text block, type is broken into segments and placed throughout the design to create a hierarchy that compliments the treatment of the images.

Asymmetrical column-based grid

Asymmetrical module-based grid

Client: Office of the Deputy Prime Minister
Design: Cartlidge Levene
Layout synopsis: Asymmetrical grid and columns to organise complex cross-referencing information

Towns & Cities, Partners in Urban Renaissance

This four-volume document, *Towns & Cities, Partners in Urban Renaissance,* was designed by Cartlidge Levene for the Office of the Deputy Prime Minister in the UK.

Each volume features a plain cover that is cut short to reveal a full-colour image underneath. The design uses an asymmetrical grid, with the left-hand column employed as a wide margin. The main body copy in each book is set in a warm grey and each book also uses a secondary text colour. This secondary colour is used to highlight pull-quotes and also to indicate passages that relate to other volumes in the document. Simplified typographical control – use of indents, colour, text rules and weights – provide sufficient variation to aid navigation.

This understated and controlled layout provides ample space around the text, creating a peaceful 'area' that helps the reader tackle complex information and also provides a convenient space for notes.

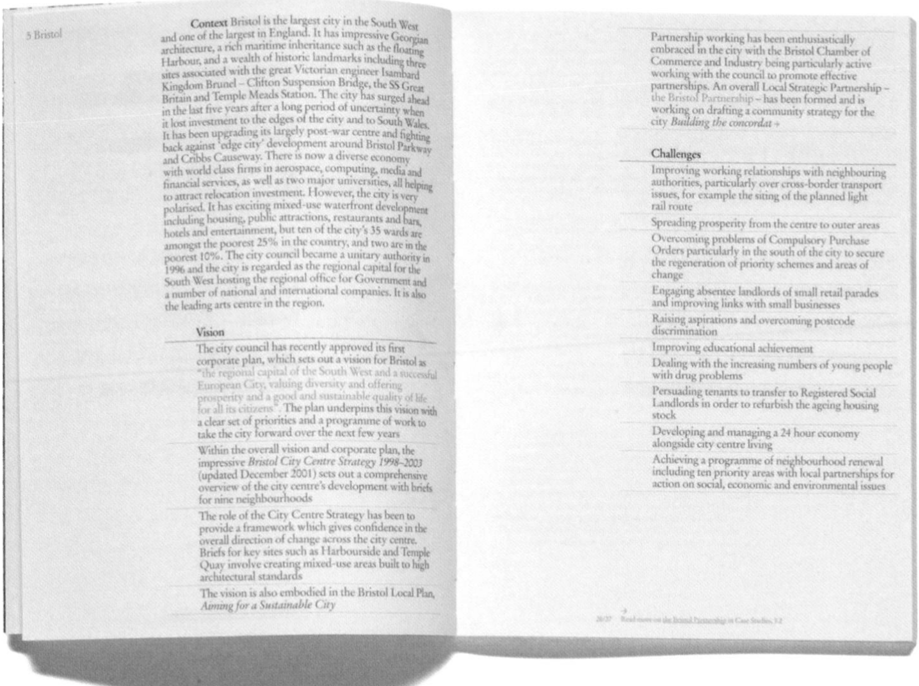

5 Bristol

Context Bristol is the largest city in the South West and one of the largest in England. It has impressive Georgian architecture, a rich maritime inheritance such as the floating Harbour, and a wealth of historic landmarks including three sites associated with the great Victorian engineer Isambard Kingdom Brunel – Clifton Suspension Bridge, the SS Great Britain and Temple Meads Station. The city has surged ahead in the last five years after a long period of uncertainty when it lost investment to the edges of the city and to South Wales. It has been upgrading its largely post-war centre and fighting back against 'edge city' development around Bristol Parkway and Cribbs Causeway. There is now a diverse economy with world class firms in aerospace, computing, media and financial services, as well as two major universities, all helping to attract relocation investment. However, the city is very polarised. It has exciting mixed-use waterfront development including housing, public attractions, restaurants and bars, hotels and entertainment, but ten of the city's 35 wards are amongst the poorest 25% in the country, and two are in the poorest 10%. The city council became a unitary authority in 1996 and the city is regarded as the regional capital for the South West hosting the regional office for Government and a number of national and international companies. It is also the leading arts centre in the region.

Vision

The city council has recently approved its first corporate plan, which sets out a vision for Bristol as "the regional capital of the South West and a successful European City, valuing diversity and offering prosperity and a good and sustainable quality of life for all its citizens". The plan underpins this vision with a clear set of priorities and a programme of work to take the city forward over the next few years

Within the overall vision and corporate plan, the impressive *Bristol City Centre Strategy 1998–2003* (updated December 2001) sets out a comprehensive overview of the city centre's development with briefs for nine neighbourhoods

The role of the City Centre Strategy has been to provide a framework which gives confidence in the overall direction of change across the city centre. Briefs for key sites such as Harbourside and Temple Quay involve creating mixed-use areas built to high architectural standards

The vision is also embodied in the Bristol Local Plan, *Aiming for a Sustainable City*

Partnership working has been enthusiastically embraced in the city with the Bristol Chamber of Commerce and Industry being particularly active working with the council to promote effective partnerships. An overall Local Strategic Partnership – the Bristol Partnership – has been formed and is working on drafting a community strategy for the city *Building the concordat* →

Challenges

Improving working relationships with neighbouring authorities, particularly over cross-border transport issues, for example the siting of the planned light rail route

Spreading prosperity from the centre to outer areas

Overcoming problems of Compulsory Purchase Orders particularly in the south of the city to secure the regeneration of priority schemes and areas of change

Engaging absentee landlords of small retail parades and improving links with small businesses

Raising aspirations and overcoming postcode discrimination

Improving educational achievement

Dealing with the increasing numbers of young people with drug problems

Persuading tenants to transfer to Registered Social Landlords in order to refurbish the ageing housing stock

Developing and managing a 24 hour economy alongside city centre living

Achieving a programme of neighbourhood renewal including ten priority areas with local partnerships for action on social, economic and environmental issues

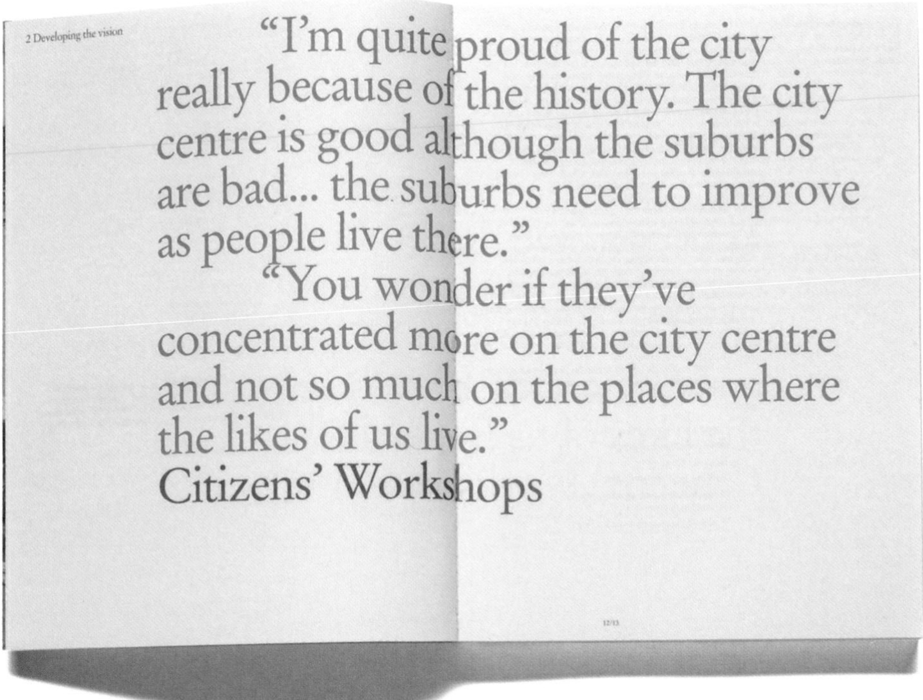

2 Developing the vision

"I'm quite proud of the city really because of the history. The city centre is good although the suburbs are bad... the suburbs need to improve as people live there."

"You wonder if they've concentrated more on the city centre and not so much on the places where the likes of us live."

Citizens' Workshops

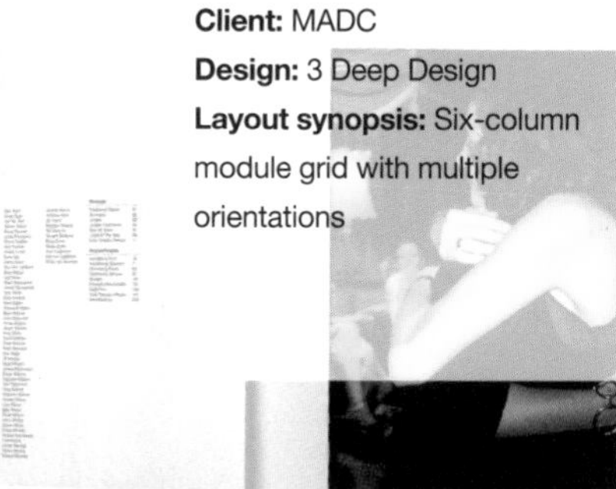

Client: MADC

Design: 3 Deep Design

Layout synopsis: Six-column module grid with multiple orientations

MADC 2002 (left)

This brochure for the Melbourne Advertising and Design Club by 3 Deep Design uses a six-column grid. The cover clearly displays six columns and an overprinted title (bottom left) inside; the columns are broken down to form modules. This provides a wider range of options for text and image placement and allows text to run-in vertically and horizontally. The six-column grid can be broken into different configurations. In the main spreads (left) the body text occupies the width of two columns; a further column is left blank providing a space between the title and the information.

AA Peter Markli (right)

Frost Design used a simple structure to create this strong layout to deal with the architectural content of the book. Recto pages have titles running at 90 degrees top to bottom, whilst on verso pages they run bottom to top. Images appear full-bleed on three sides (top row, left), passe partout (middle row, left), bleeding bottom (middle row, right) and bleeding top (bottom row, right).

Client: AA Peter Markli
Design: Frost Design
Layout synopsis: Multiple orientations and varied image bleeds

Shakespeare approximates the remote, and familiarizes the wonderful. Johnson

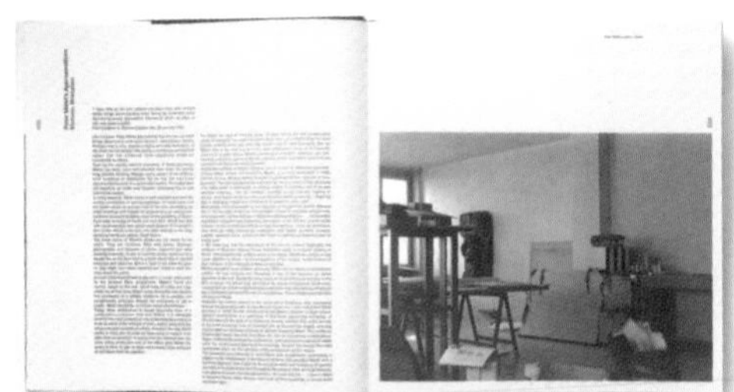

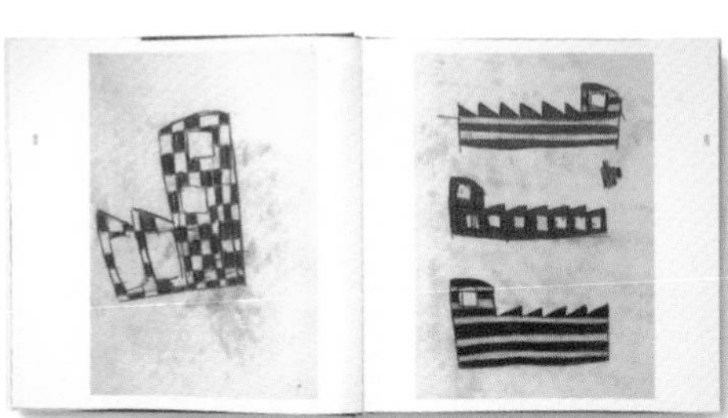

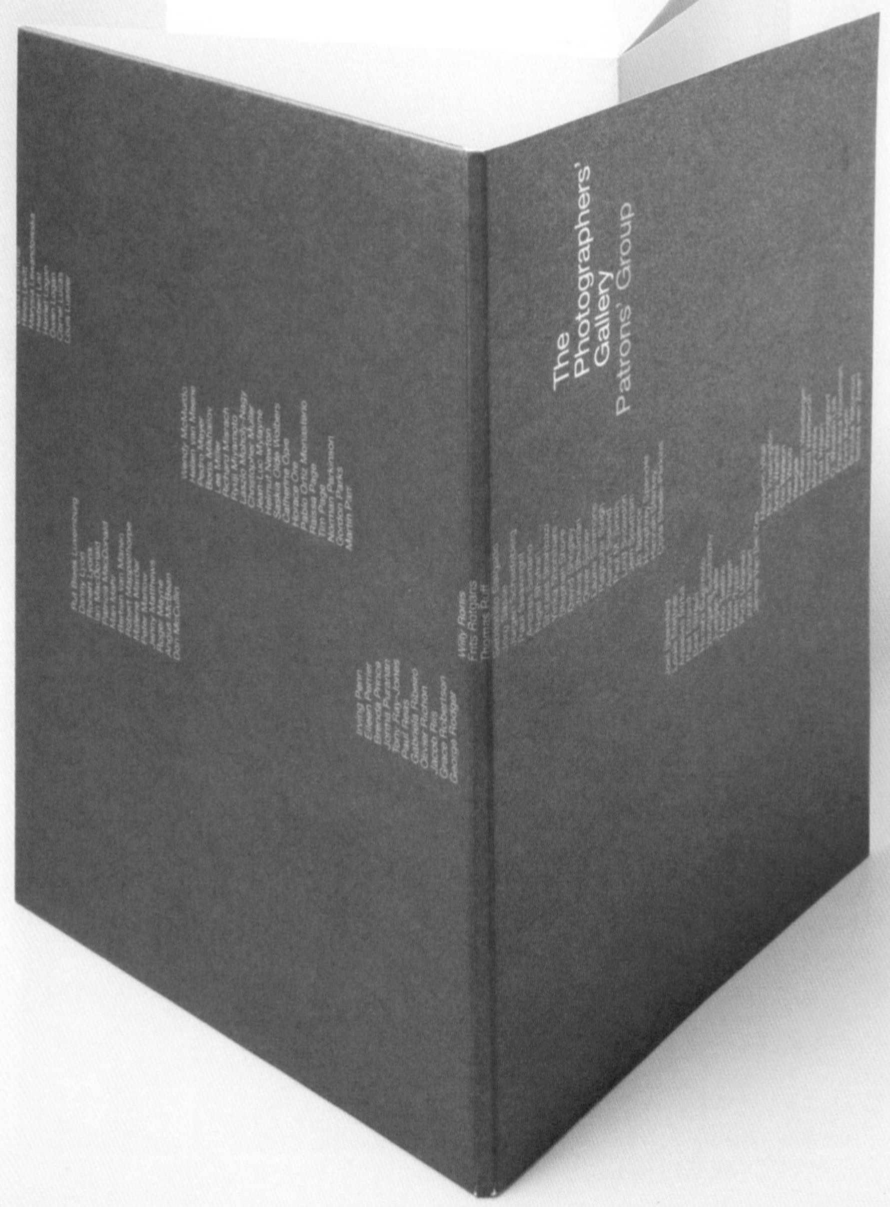

Client:
The Photographers' Gallery
Design: North
Layout synopsis: Vertical stress for body text, horizontal for titles

The Photographers' Gallery

This eight-page pack for The Photographers' Gallery's patrons group has a vertically orientated layout rather than adopting the standard horizontal approach. Body text runs vertically, whilst titles run horizontally at the foot of the page. This is an unusual treatment as titles are traditionally positioned at the top of the page, but as the body text runs vertically the larger point size and horizontal orientation of these titles makes them stand out clearly.

The placement of text blocks is dictated by the band of images passing through the lower portion of each page. Different sized images allow the use of varied text measures to create stark blocks in the layout. Photographs have a common baseline that divides the page and allows space for titles.

Developing the grid

So far we have looked at column- or module-based grids as a key design tool. It is common for designers to use both simultaneously, producing a grid that is flexible enough to hold text columns and different image configurations.

The grid below is based on a 5 x 6 arrangement of modules, each of which further subdivides into 16 smaller fields. The baseline grid (indicated by the magenta lines at the outer edge of the page) corresponds to these modules. Vertical column guides (in cyan) and horizontal 'hanging' or 'drop' lines provide hook points for image and text block placement.

This grid can be used in many different configurations (shown opposite); it provides consistency but does not force a rigid, staid or static appearance. The grid allows a plethora of possibilities and, as such, guides placement decisions rather than presents constraints.

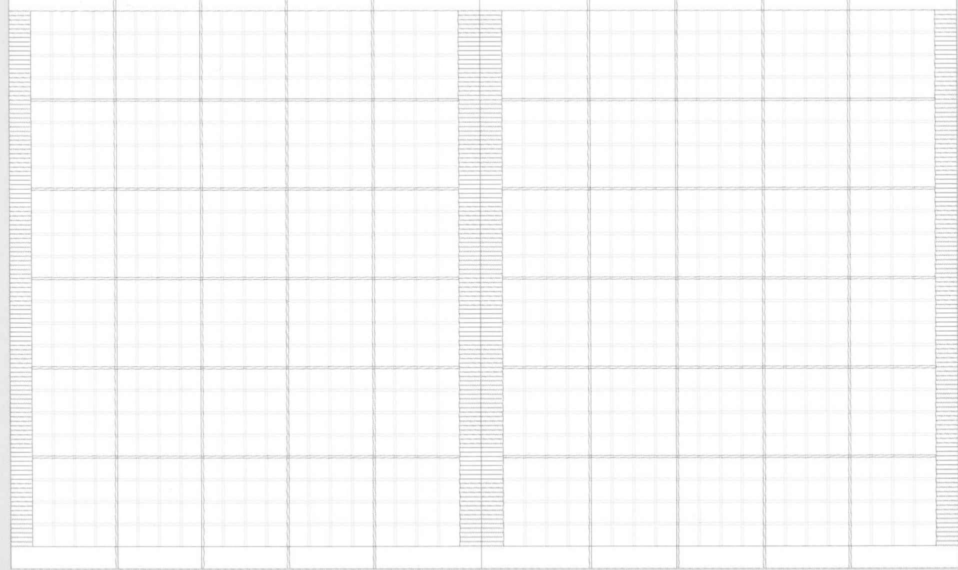

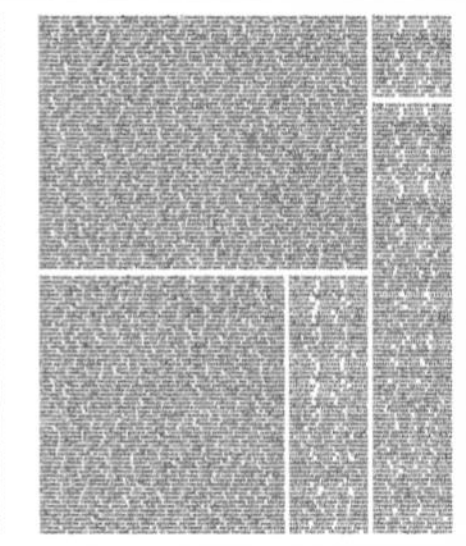

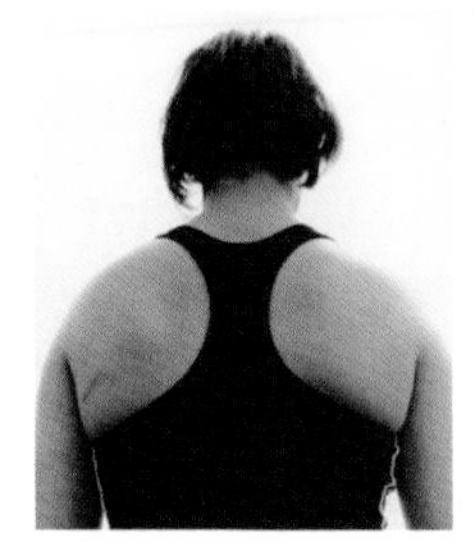

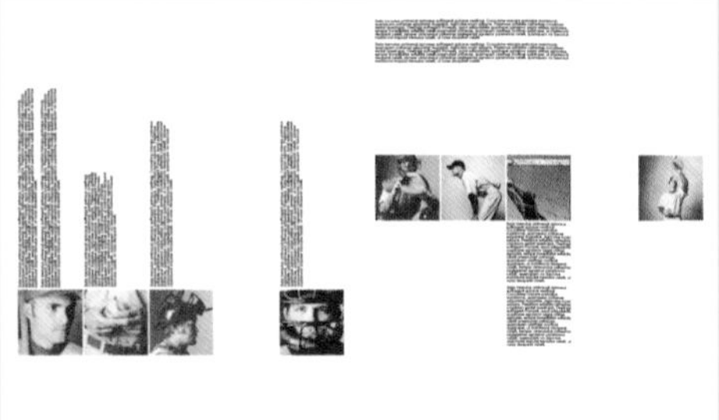

Clockwise from top left: Narrow or wide measures can be accommodated; irregular text blocks are configured using the column guides and hanging lines; multiple images with text aligned from a hanging line; full-bleed image; five-column grid; text aligned with hanging lines; vertical running text; image presented passe partout with body text/caption configuration.

Scene by Scene

Pictured are spreads from *Scene by Scene*; a book by Mark Cousins. The pages have a three-column structure with modules that correspond to the dimensions of a cinema-film frame. This grid is used to create divider spreads for each decade or chapter, which also serves as a miniature contents page.

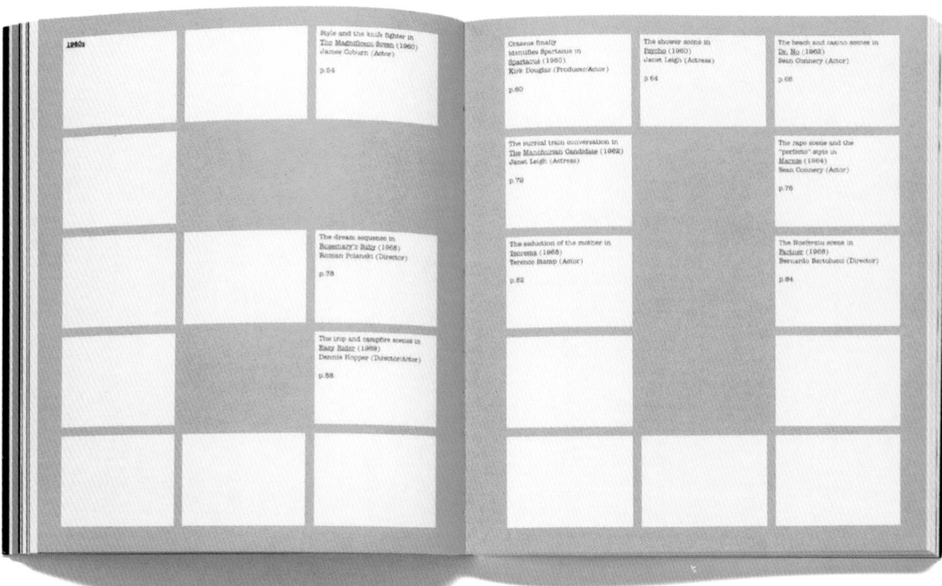

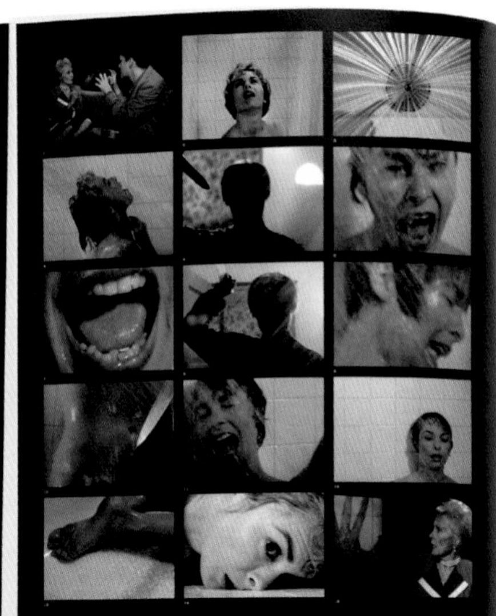

Client: Laurence King

Design: NB: Studio

Layout synopsis: Modular three-column symmetrical grid

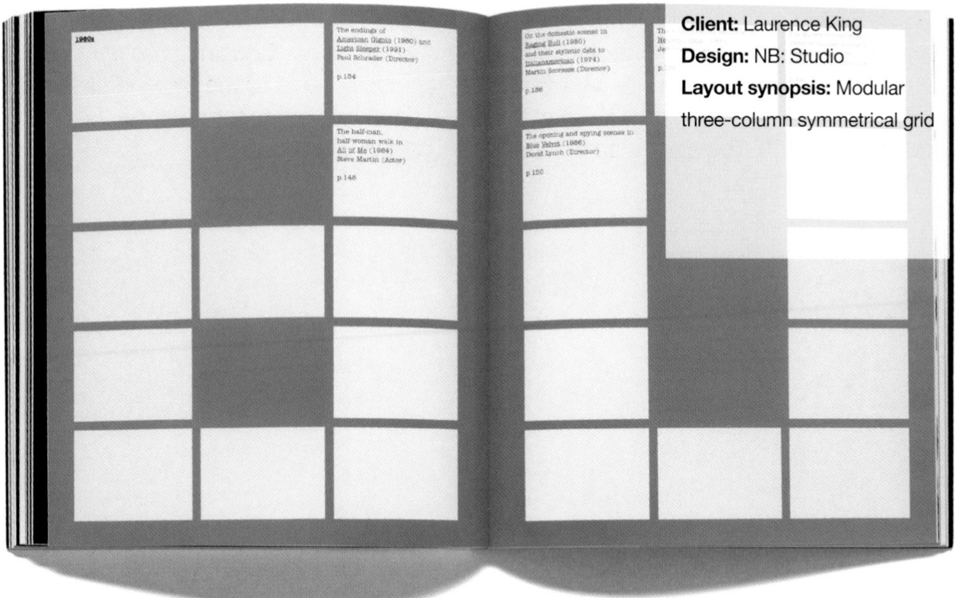

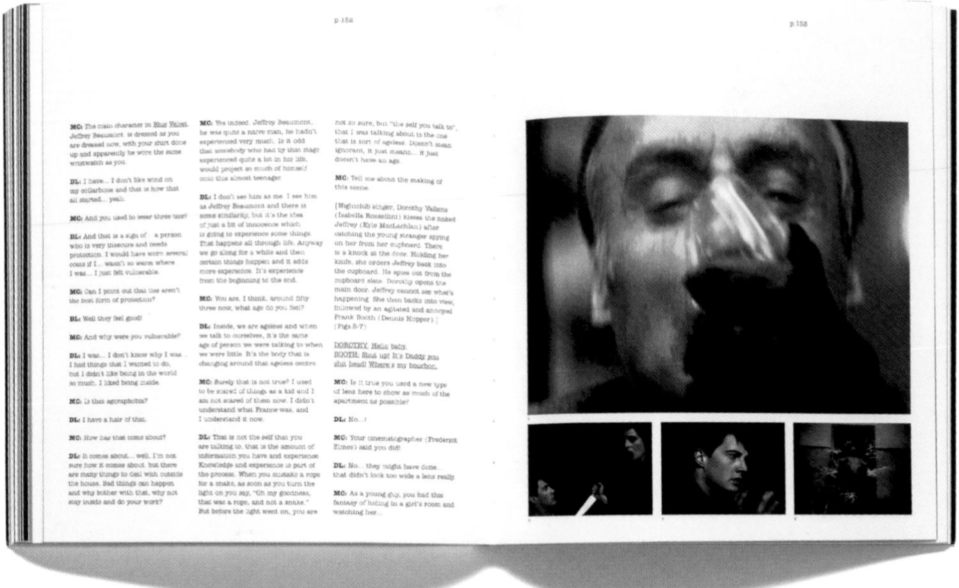

The grid allows for consistent image placement and yet offers variation. As the spreads demonstrate, the 15 modules are easily reduced to four (above). This layout enables images to be used without cropping and the repeated use of the modular grid reinforces the cinematic theme. All type is set in a monospaced typewriter font – with one size and only two weights in order to echo the aesthetics of a script – and is enforced with solid space returns and underlined titles.

1980-2001

Client: Conran & Partners

Design: Studio Myerscough

Layout synopsis: Two-column symmetrical grid

NO HOUSE STYLE BUT A HISTORY. NOT A FIXED POSITION, BUT A FOCUS ON QUESTIONING WHAT GOES ON WHEN ONE TAKES A JOURNEY FROM PAST TO PRESENT. WHAT PROCESS OF CHANGE OCCURS? WHY MIGHT ONE WANT TO CHANGE? THIS BOOK AIMS TO EXPLORE THE WORK OF A GLOBAL, MULTI-DISCIPLINARY ARCHITECTURAL PRACTICE. EVOLVED OVER 21 YEARS, CONRAN & PARTNERS' ARCHITECTURE, URBAN AND INTERIOR DESIGN ADHERES TO A COMMITMENT TO WHAT ARCHITECTURAL CRITIC DEYAN SUDJIC CALLS "MAKING PLACES THAT ARE ALIVE".

The images in this spread are very tight and ordered in contrast with the spacious treatment given over to the typesetting. The white borders in which the images are set suggest a window frame so that the reader feels as if they are looking into the interiors.

The Grid

The grid is a means of positioning and containing the elements of a design in order to facilitate and ease decision making. Using a grid results in a more considered approach and allows greater accuracy in the placement of page elements, either in terms of physical measurements or proportional space.

Grids have varying degrees of complexity and so can provide for a vast number of design and positioning possibilities. By providing coherency to a design, a grid allows a designer to use their time efficiently and concentrate on achieving a successful design.

A grid allows the designer to make informed decisions, which eliminates the random placement of elements and helps to ensure that the various components work together within the overall design. A grid can be used to reflect the nature of the content and/or the size and proportion of the page.

However, dogmatically adhering to the structure of a grid can stifle creativity and result in designs that demonstrate little imagination. Although a grid can guide layout decisions, it is not considered to be a complete substitute for making them.

'The reduction of the number of visual elements used and their incorporation in a grid system creates a sense of compact planning, intelligibility and clarity, and suggests orderliness of design. The orderliness lends added credibility to the information and induces confidence.'
Josef Müller-Brockmann

From Milton Keynes to Manhattan (left)

This brochure for Conran & Partners by Studio Myerscough is based on a symmetrical two-column grid that clearly reflects the positions of the two text blocks (opposite, top). This is varied by using single text columns (middle, left). The breaker pages (middle, right) use a visible hairline grid as a feature.

Most designers use a grid to produce a piece of work, which will usually be invisible in the finished design. The grid can be made visible by drawing lines over it to incorporate it into the piece. Showing the scaffold with which the design was created conveys an obvious sense of order, which is appropriate for the architectural/interiors example shown opposite.

The baseline grid

The baseline grid is the graphic foundation upon which a design is constructed. It serves a similar supporting role as the scaffolding used in building construction. The baseline grid provides a guide for positioning elements on the page with accuracy, which is difficult to achieve by eye alone.

These three text blocks use different typefaces and point sizes but they all lock to the same baseline grid. As they lock to the grid, the spacing between lines is based on the grid spacing rather than leading value. Left to right the fonts are: Hoefler Text 6.5pt, 55 Helvetica Roman 7.5pt and GeoSlab712 10pt.

These three text blocks use different typefaces and point sizes but they all lock to the same baseline grid. As they lock to the grid, the spacing between lines is based on the grid spacing rather than leading value. Left to right the fonts are: Hoefler Text 6.5pt, 55 Helvetica Roman 7.5pt and GeoSlab712 10pt.

These three text blocks use different typefaces and point sizes but they all lock to the same baseline grid. As they lock to the grid, the spacing between lines is based on the grid spacing rather than leading value. Left to right the fonts are: Hoefler Text 6.5pt, 55 Helvetica Roman 7.5pt and GeoSlab712 10pt.

Baseline

Type is positioned to sit on the baseline of the grid. Some characters, such as the ‘o’, are slightly larger in order to maintain a consistent visual effect because they would appear to be smaller if they were cut to the same proportions as other letters. To compensate for its larger size, the ‘o’ sits slightly below the baseline.

This text block is set in a baseline grid (in magenta) whose lines are 24pt apart. Any combination of type sizes and leading values can be used if the sum results in 24pt.

Shown below are some examples of how this works:

Below left: the heading or titling is set 24pt solid.
(One line of copy at 24pt set solid = 24pt)

Below middle: body copy is set 10pt on + 2pt leading. This means that the two lines of this body copy coupled with its leading is equal to 24pts. It therefore fits in the baseline grid and corresponds to one line of the heading copy.
(Two lines of copy at 10pt + 2pt additional leading = 24pt)

Below right: captioning is set 7pt on + 1pt leading.
(Three lines of copy at 7pt + 1pt additional leading = 24pt)

This title is set in 24pt, solid.

One line of this type fills one line of the grid.

This body copy is set as 10pt Sabon Regular on + 2pt leading. This means that the two lines of this body copy coupled with its leading is equal to 24pt and therefore fits in the baseline grid.

One line of heading, two lines of body copy or three lines of captions extend for the same depth down the column.

These captions are set in 7pt type with + 1pt of leading. They use an italic to create a more visible differentiation.

Three lines at 7pt set with + 1pt leading per line equals 24pt, therefore three lines of captions will align with two lines of body copy and one line of title type.

Client: Van Kranendonk Art Projects
Design: Faydherbe / De Vringer
Layout synopsis: Exposed baseline grid, text block has same measure as passe partout

A Wide View Up Close

This is a book featuring images of eight farmers and their farms by Dutch photographer Wijnanda Deroo. The photographs are accompanied by interviews from Fred van Wijnen, which are intended to provide an insight into life on a farm.

The baseline grid was included in the design as a series of faint white lines and gives an interesting mechanical juxtaposition to the pastoral images contained in the book. The inclusion of the grid shows how the various text elements are located and how they relate to each other. The outer boundary of the text block, formed by the grid, corresponds to the passe partout that is used to frame the photographs.

Cross-alignment
In this context cross-alignment refers to establishing a typographical hierarchy whereby the different textual levels share a common relationship and as such can be used and aligned in the same grid, as shown in the example opposite. Leading is used both to space text lines and to ensure that alignment is possible.

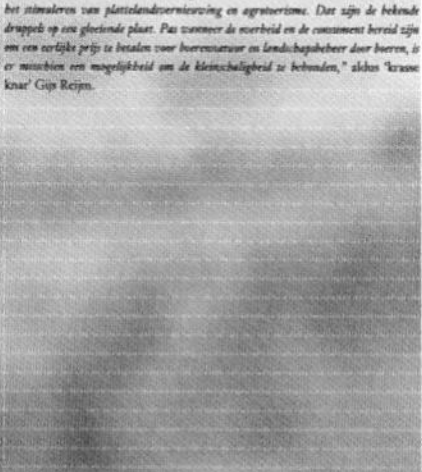

Burt Zuidbroek (jr.):

Cows, cheese, and pigs

Marinus Rooken:

Attached to the Krimpenerwaard

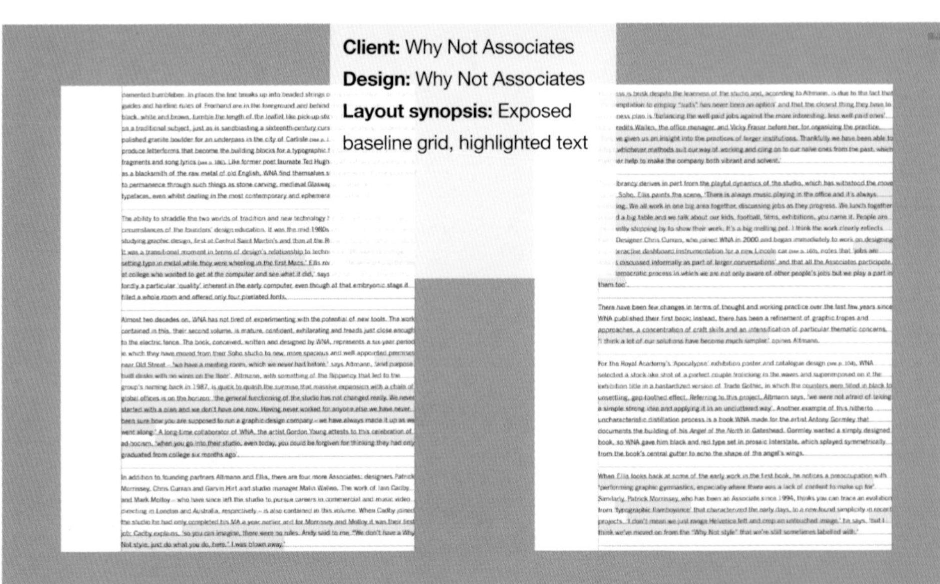

Client: Why Not Associates

Design: Why Not Associates

Layout synopsis: Exposed baseline grid, highlighted text

Why Not Associates Book 2

This book, designed by Why Not Associates, uses an exposed baseline grid and highlighted text to provide dynamic touches to the design. Showing the nuts and bolts of the designer's craft for page construction here (top), contrasts dramatically with the space and freedom of the image-based spreads (bottom).

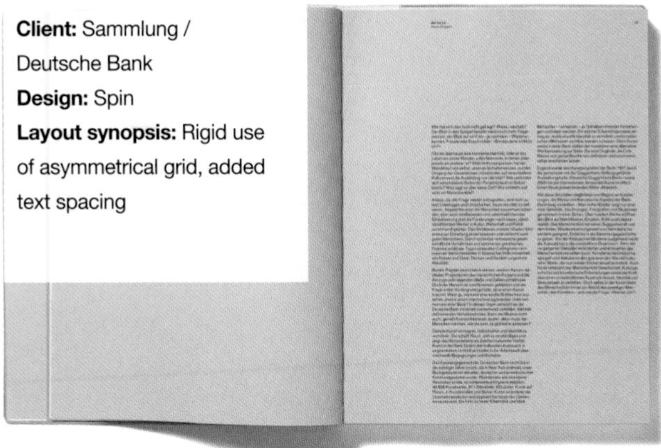

Client: Sammlung / Deutsche Bank
Design: Spin
Layout synopsis: Rigid use of asymmetrical grid, added text spacing

Man in the Middle

This publication forms part of the Deutsche Bank art project.
A rigid, asymmetrical-baseline grid is used to order type and image placement so that title cap heights, captions and images all align (bottom). Text in the yellow spread is set with additional spacing, which creates subtle differences that break up the formal structure imposed by the grid (centre).

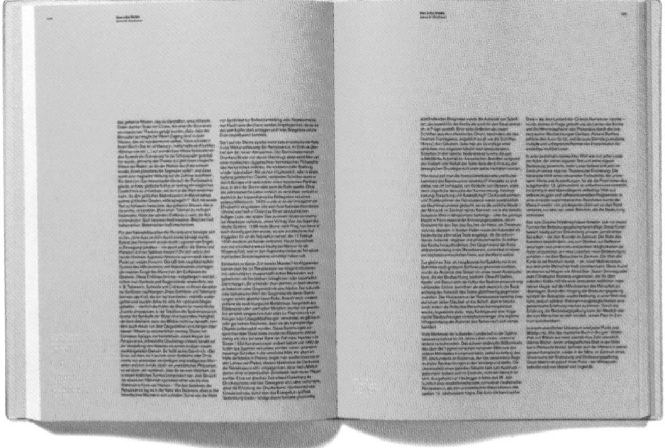

There columns of images (left) are spread across the page and butt up against one another without adhering to the widths of the text columns.

Images

Images are the graphic elements that can bring a design to life. Whether as the main focus of a page or as a subsidiary element, images play an essential role in communicating a message and are thus a vital factor in establishing the visual identity of a piece of work.

Images can be incorporated into a design in many ways, as shown in the examples throughout this volume, from full-bleed and passe partout to positioning using a variety of grid systems.

Basic layout principles help the designer to use images in a consistent manner and in such a way that they remain in harmony with the other elements of the design.

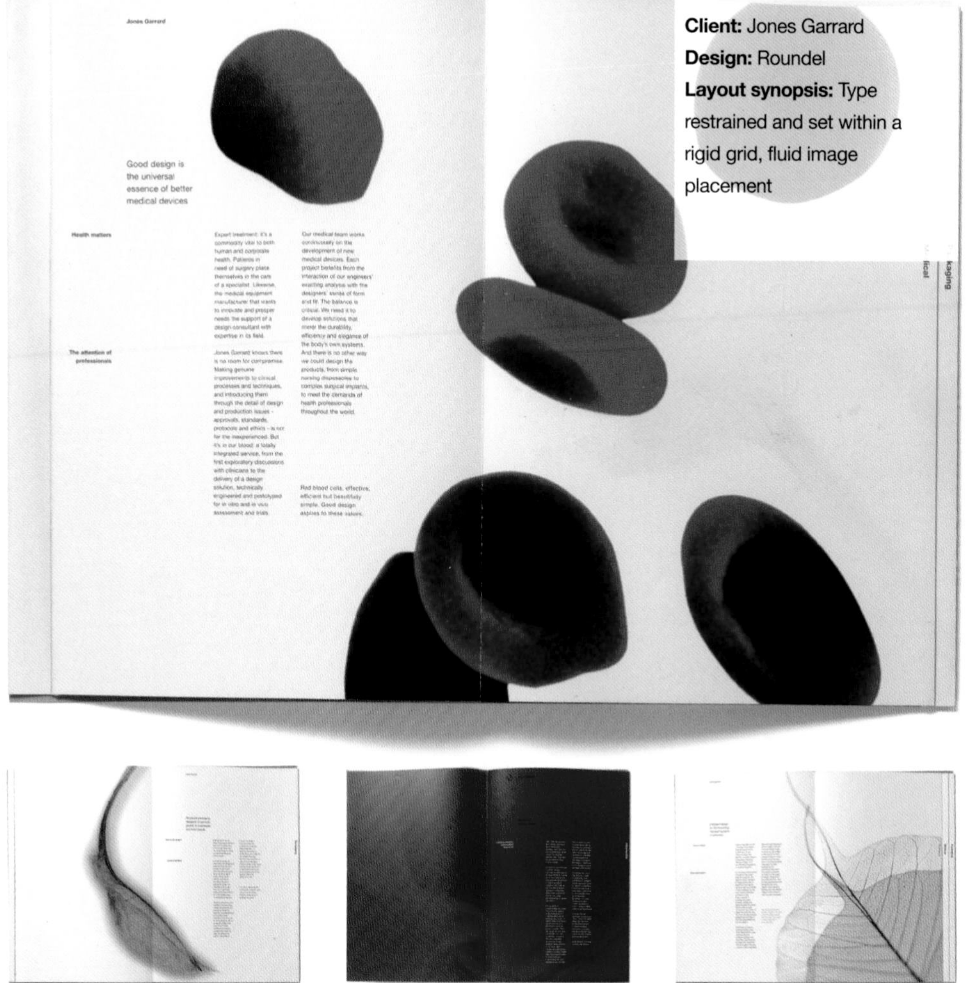

Client: Jones Garrard
Design: Roundel
Layout synopsis: Type restrained and set within a rigid grid, fluid image placement

Jones Garrard

This brochure for Jones Garrard by Roundel features type that is restrained and set in narrow columns within a rigid grid. This is accompanied by very fluid image placement.

The positioning of the type provides continuity and allows for variation without the design appearing random. Images that bleed off the page add raw dynamism to the spreads. Titles are positioned to the far right and pull-quotes are set in a larger typeface above and away from the body copy.

The pages of this concertina-fold document are cut incrementally narrower so that the reader can see the edge of the preceding and subsequent pages. This allows you to see the titles of all the pages within the brochure immediately.

Client: 45 Tabernacle Street
Design: Form Design
Layout synopsis: Simple vertical grid with a column of images and a column of text

45 Tabernacle Street

This simple single-fold mailer by Form Design for a property development in London uses a simple vertical grid. Images are placed in one column, with the supporting text in the adjacent column. This straightforward information structure harmonises with the understated simplicity of the development.

45 Tabernacle Street **is a five-storey apartment building in the heart of Shoreditch. The development comprises three one-bedroom apartments, and one two-storey penthouse, each individually conceived and designed, with bespoke fittings and high quality contemporary furniture. The apartments are set apart by their unique character. Each one incorporates a different combination of carefully considered space planning, colours, materials and finishes.**

1st Floor
Theme: Contemporary Loft
The first floor apartment has a relaxed theme executed in a live-work style. The interior includes natural oak flooring, stainless steel, white lacquered storage units and frosted glass to create a cool contemporary feel. Exposed brickwork and original structural elements add to the character of relaxed minimal design. A bathroom floor paved in grey slate complements white glass tiling and chrome fittings. Stainless steel and aluminium complete the pared down palette in the kitchen.

2nd Floor
Theme: Contemporary Sport
A fun, sporting theme for the second floor encompasses narrow strip grey stained oak flooring, bespoke cabinetry - silvery grey on the outside and a rich scarlet on the inside, and a screen to the bedroom area of grey felt stitched in red. Kitchen cupboards and appliances are faced in a deep blue rubberized surface and finished with a stainless steel worktop. Green slate flooring, frosted glass tiles and chrome fittings complete the crisp interior of the bathroom.

3rd Floor
Theme: Contemporary Calm
A pared down palette of materials; polished plaster, narrow strip maple flooring, white lacquer and glass combine to create a contemplative interior on the 3rd floor. The bedroom is screened from the main living area by an elegant frameless, floor to ceiling screen of white glass. White lacquered cabinets fitted with roller blind shutters enable storage areas and the entertainment system to be hidden from view. The kitchen is finished in white lacquer whilst limestone floors and walls in the bathroom complete this calming environment.

Penthouse
Theme: Luxurious Minimalism
Natural light pours into the penthouse through a dramatic wall of sloping glass looking out over Tabernacle Street. The lower section of the glazing is powered and lifts to provide a balcony the full width of the building. The spacious living and dining space on the lower floor is laid with herringbone Wenge parquet flooring, rich in colour and complemented by the black lacquer and stainless steel kitchen. A cloakroom and small bathroom complete facilities on the lower floor.

Accessed by a stainless steel spiral staircase, the upper mezzanine area spans half the apartment and houses the bedroom and main bathroom. Polished plaster surfaces in this area reflect the plentiful light on the mezzanine whilst grey slate and limestone surfaces are applied to the 'wet-room' environment of the bathroom, which houses a drench shower and a sunken jacuzzi amongst other unique designs.

Common themes

Throughout
- Italian and bespoke furniture to complement the individual theme of each space
- Modular recessed lighting, fully programmable Lutron controls, integrated with audio system
- Alessi china and cookware
- Broadband internet access via wireless LAN
- Gas central heating

Living area
- Solid hardwood flooring
- Integrated Bang and Olufsen audio and telephone system including satellite TV

Kitchen
- Top of the range Boffi kitchen with Kupperbusch oven and hob
- Washer/dryer
- Fridge-freezer
- Dishwasher

Bathroom
- Under floor heating
- High pressure water
- Luxury sanitary ware with jacuzzi
- High quality fittings

Bedroom
- Bespoke bedroom furniture and fittings
- Full height double doors to balcony

Balcony
- Hardwood decked balcony

Entrance and lobby area
- 'Keyless' security door opening system
- Lacquered natural oak flooring
- Automatically controlled recessed lighting and stunning wall artwork
- Steel staircase access to apartments with full height glazing, flooding common areas with natural light

This baseline grid has lines that are 10pt apart. The bottom of the image is positioned against the baseline of the text, a common practice as it ensures a clean sight line between the text and the image. The 21 lines of text in this column are set 8pt + 2pt leading to fit to the grid.

When the images have been placed and the text flowed in, the resulting page appears as a series of boxes, modules or fields. In the layout for this page, each image is accompanied by a corresponding text block that has the same dimensions.

Whilst this produces a design that is neat and coherent, over successive pages it can become stifling and difficult to read – particularly if there is a single body of text that is flowed throughout the section or document.

Client: Citibank Private Bank
Design: North
Layout synopsis: High image placement, right-hand bleed instils movement

Citibank Private Bank Photography Prize

This is the catalogue for the Citibank Private Bank Photography Prize 2001 by North design studio. Images and type are used to subtly imply a sense of movement throughout the book.

The placement of these stark images enhances their drama. Positioning the images high up the page with a narrow top margin and broad bottom margin adds intensity. By bleeding off the right-hand edge there is a sense of horizontal movement as one spread connects with the next at the turn of the page.

The Tables Turned

Jeremy Millar

Let me presume, dear reader, that you are currently standing within The Photographers' Gallery, and have visited, or are in the process of visiting, the Citibank Private Bank Photography Prize 2001, of which the publication you are now reading is the accompanying catalogue. Perhaps you are standing in the foyer, leafing through a copy by the reception desk, or perhaps you are standing in the bookshop, fingers and eyes skimming across pictures, sliding along words. Perhaps you've even bought this copy and are now sitting in the café and are at this minute reading these very words. Now, can I ask you to put the book down and follow me outside, (or bring it with you, if it's yours). You can come back in afterwards, that's fine. Go out through the door, the glass opening out onto a street thick with noise and metallic air, and move towards your left. If you've come from the bookshop, you'll have to walk a bit further, until you are in front of the gallery's other building. Now, mindful of other pedestrians, turn to face the building and you will see, above your head, caught in the black tile grid, a blue plaque on which you can read: 'Sir Joshua Reynolds — Artist — Lived Here 1753–1761'.

The intervening essay sections, although typographically restrained, also convey this sense of movement. A deep indentation of the essay title and author name suggest left-to-right movement in the texts. This is reinforced further by the use of the longer em dash instead of the more familiar and shorter en dash.

These typographic techniques establish a hierarchy that instils a sense of order and also adds to the dynamism and movement of the publication.

Client: Tourism Victoria
Design: 3 Deep Design
Layout synopsis: Full-bleed images with minimal text intervention

Elements on a Page

Text and images are the key components a layout is used to organise so as to present them to the reader in such a way that they communicate effectively. A design's ability to communicate is influenced by the position of the text and images in relation to other elements, what the focal point of the page is, type alignment and how white space is treated.

The intensity of the arrangement and the amount of free space surrounding the text and image elements are key design considerations. Many designers often feel compelled to fill this space rather than use it as another feature of a design. Tight positioning of elements can give a design a more frenetic pace, while introducing space can produce greater tranquillity, as the examples opposite show.

'Perfection is achieved, not when there is nothing more to add, but when there is nothing left to take away.'
Antoine de Saint-Exupéry

Tourism Victoria (left)

This brochure for Tourism Victoria by 3 Deep Design has little apparent structure due to the preference given over to the images. The cover text 'Melbourne, Victoria, Australia' on the front and 'open, discover, explore' on the back are printed as a spot varnish. Inside the brochure stark greyscale imagery has minimal captioning and intervening white pages break the pace of the document.

Alignment

Alignment refers to the position of type within a text block, in both the vertical and horizontal planes.

Vertical alignment
This is the vertical alignment of text in the field and can be centred, top or bottom.

Horizontal alignment
This is the horizontal alignment of text in the field and can be range left, range right, centred or justified.

Top aligned/range left/ragged right
The text in this example has been vertically aligned to the top of the field. As the text is ranged left it automatically creates a ragged-right edge.

Bottom aligned/range left
The text in this example has been aligned to the bottom of the field.

Top aligned/range right/ragged left
The text in this example has been vertically aligned to the top of the field and ranged right to leave a ragged-left edge.

Vertically centred alignment/ centred text
The text in this example is centred in the measure. This can be difficult to read as the starting point for each line is irregular.

Top aligned/centred text
The text in this example is centred in the measure and aligned to the top.

Bottom aligned/centred text
The text in this example is centred in the measure and aligned to the bottom.

Horizontal and vertical justification
Justified text is extended across the measure aligning on both the left and right margins. In narrow measures this can create gaps, which over successive text lines may result in rivers. Poorly justified text can result in words being broken in irregular places. However, it is generally considered preferable to break a word, rather than create an exaggerated space by pushing it over (returning it) to a new line. Justifying text vertically can produce an adverse effect as more or less leading will appear to have been added to the text block as the lines stretch or contract to fit.

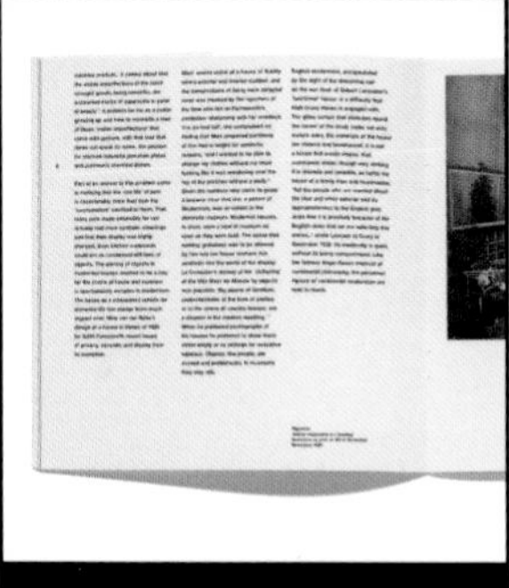

Pages 34–35

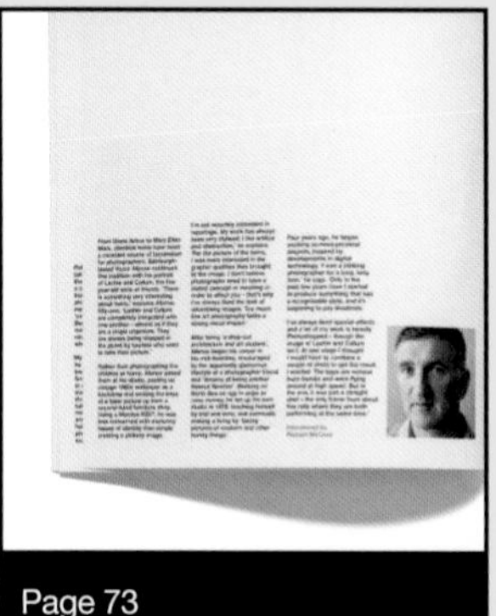

Page 73

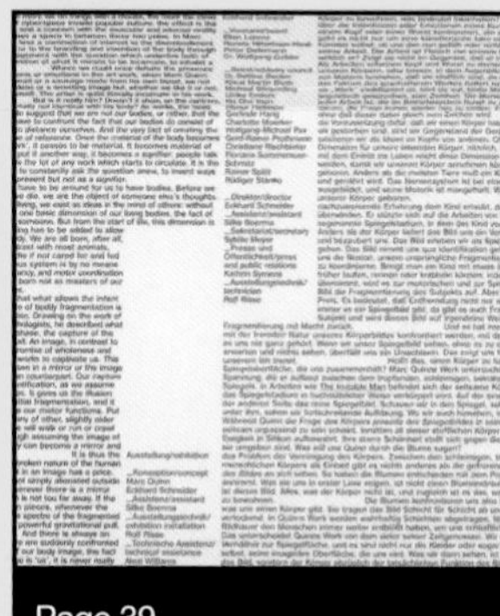

Page 39

Top aligned
This three-column spread has text that is aligned from a hanging line. Top alignment provides a formal and consistent layout of text.

Bottom aligned
This three-column spread has text that is aligned to the bottom of the foot margin. Although unconventional, this method can add dynamism to the page.

Range left (ragged right)
The text in this example is range left leaving a ragged-right edge. This ragged edge needs to be carefully returned to ensure that there are no words left isolated.

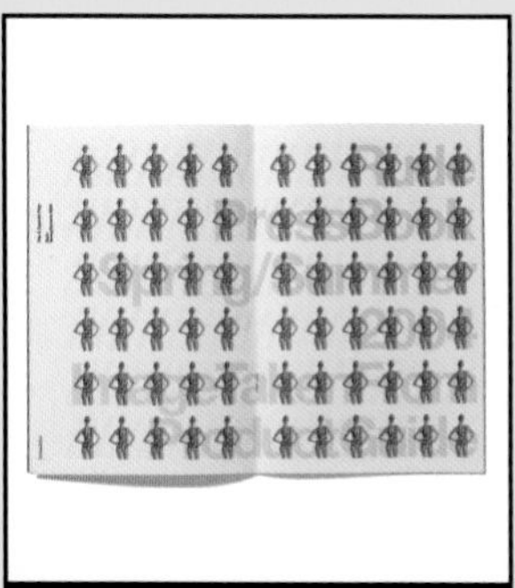

Page 85

Page 101

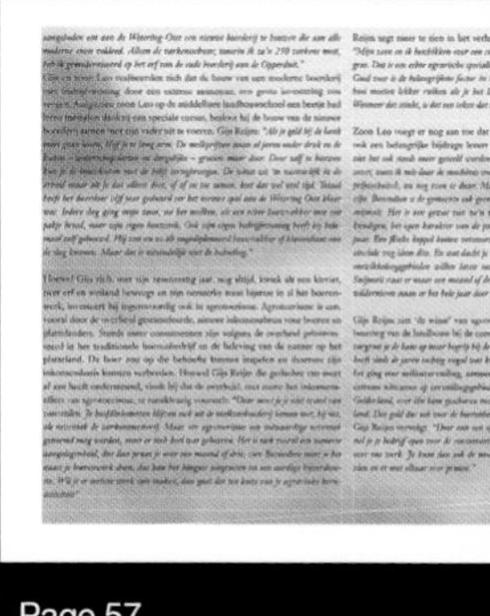

Page 57

Range right (ragged left)
The text in this example is range right to leave a ragged-left edge. Far less common than range left, as the eye uses the strong left-hand vertical line to read from. The fragmented feel that this gives, although not successful for body text, can work well for display type.

Centred
This heading is centred in both the horizontal and vertical planes. As a general rule, centred text when used as body copy can be unnecessarily hard to read but can work well for titles or headers.

Justified
This text is justified and results in a very formal and controlled appearance. Careful consideration needs to be given to the hyphenation and justification when setting justified type.

Client: Chamber Made Opera
Design: 3 Deep Design
Layout synopsis: Range left and range right text juxtaposition

8 Songs for a Mad King (left)

This poster by 3 Deep Design, for the Chamber Made Opera performance *8 Songs for a Mad King*, juxtaposes range right and range left text to create very eye-catching focus blocks. The design makes a feature of the single-letter widows that result from the narrow measure and large point size. The leading is set negative, making the ascenders and descenders overlap, creating an iconic, almost logo-like typography.

The Photographers' Gallery (right)

Here, the textural information is separated by point size and style. The left-hand block is plain and the right-hand block is outlined. The text blocks are range left and right respectively to further reinforce the clear difference between them.

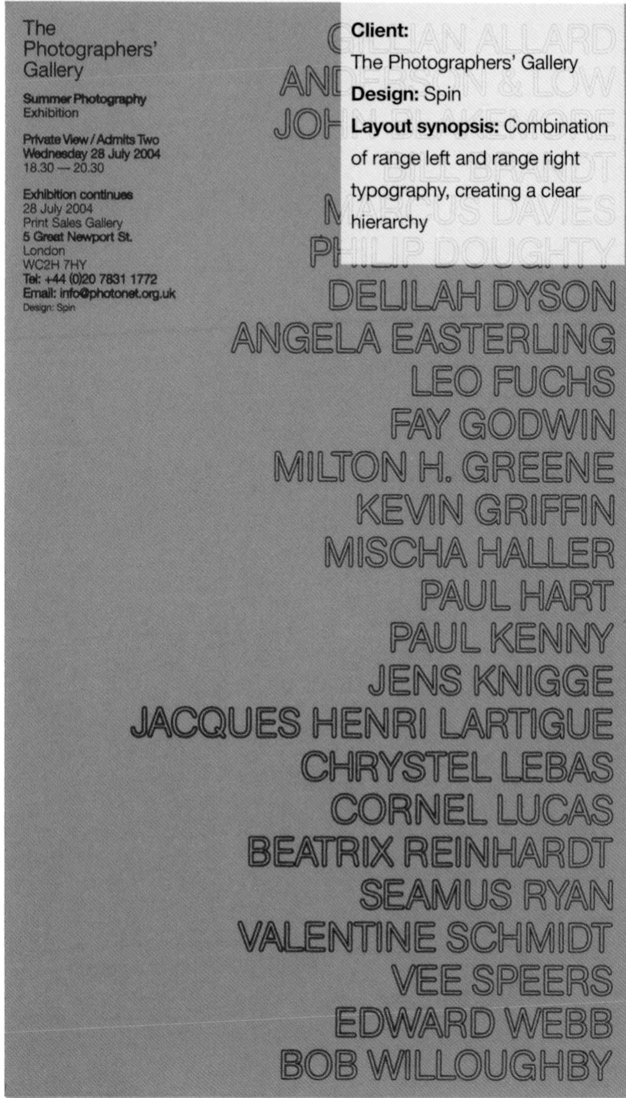

Client: The Photographers' Gallery
Design: Spin
Layout synopsis: Combination of range left and range right typography, creating a clear hierarchy

Widows and orphans
A widow is a very short line comprised of a word (or the end of a hyphenated word) at the end of a paragraph or column. An orphan is similar, the only difference is that it appears at the beginning of a column or a page.

Client: Schweppes Photographic Portrait Prize 2003
Design: NB: Studio
Layout synopsis: Text aligned from bottom, passe partout photographs

The cover flap doubles the weight of the cover and adds rigidity to it.

Schweppes Photographic Portrait Prize

Minimal titling appears on the front cover of this book documenting the *Schweppes Photographic Portrait Prize* entries. The simplicity of the text ranged right and set against a thin rule is complemented by a bright flood-printed, full-width flap that can be seen at the top and bottom of the cover.

Internally the spreads feature a series of passe partout presented photographs and large type size captioning continues the orange colour scheme. A simple hierarchy is established with the captioning top aligning and the running copy aligning at the bottom of the page. The images also align to the bottom, creating a dynamic and engaging layout with clear divisions of information.

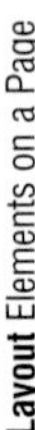

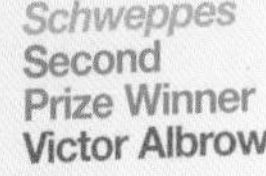

From Diane Arbus to Mary Ellen Mark, identical twins have been a constant source of fascination for photographers. Edinburgh-based Victor Albrow continues this tradition with his portrait of Lachie and Callum, the five-year-old sons of friends. 'There is something very interesting about twins,' explains Albrow, fifty-one. 'Lachie and Callum are completely integrated with one another – almost as if they are a single organism. They are always being stopped in the street by tourists who want to take their picture.'

Rather than photographing the children at home, Albrow posed them at his studio, pasting up vintage 1960s wallpaper as a backdrop and seating the boys at a table picked up from a second-hand furniture shop. Using a Mamiya RZ67, he was less concerned with exploring issues of identity than simply creating a striking image.

'I'm not remotely interested in reportage. My work has always been very stylised; I like artifice and abstraction,' he explains. 'For the picture of the twins, I was more interested in the graphic qualities they brought to the image. I don't believe photographs need to have a stated concept or meaning in order to affect you – that's why I've always liked the look of advertising images. Too much fine art photography lacks a strong visual impact.'

After being 'a drop-out architecture and art student', Albrow began his career in his mid-twenties, encouraged by the apparently glamorous lifestyle of a photographer friend and 'dreams of being another Helmut Newton'. Working on North Sea oil rigs in order to raise money, he set up his own studio in 1979, teaching himself by trial and error, and eventually making a living by 'taking pictures of cookers and other boring things'.

Four years ago, he began working on more personal projects, inspired by developments in digital technology. 'I was a jobbing photographer for a long, long time,' he says. 'Only in the past few years have I started to produce something that has a recognisable style, and it's beginning to pay dividends.

'I've always liked special effects and a lot of my work is heavily Photoshopped – though the image of Lachie and Callum isn't. At one stage I thought I would have to combine a couple of shots to get the result I wanted. The boys are serious buzz-bombs and were flying around at high speed. But in the end, it was just a straight shot – the only frame from about five rolls where they are both performing at the same time.'

Interviewed by Richard McClure

Victor Albrow Lachie and Callum May 2003

Opposite: Seamus Ryan Professor Phillip King CBE PRA May 2003

Howard John Davies Patrick July 2003

Layout Alignment

Hyphenation and justification (H&Js)

The aim of breaking words (hyphenation) is to produce text blocks that look clean and have no unsightly gaps or rivers. This is why it is important for a designer to control hyphenation.

Breaking a word should not make the text more difficult to read. Ideally it should be broken between its syllables, except for those words composed of less than four characters which should not be broken at all. The examples below demonstrate the difficulties of setting justified text in a narrow column, which requires balancing ugly spaces and a rash of hyphens. Whilst computer programs can limit the number of sequential lines that are hyphenated, they only count 'hard' hyphens that are added by the program and not the 'soft' hyphens that exist in the text (as in left-hand).

In any given piece of text, hyphenation and justification settings alter the overall appearance or 'colour' of the copy block. Word spacing, letter spacing and hyphenation settings all contribute to how a piece of text will appear.

The paragraph above is set with word spacing values of 75% minimum, 100% optimum and 150% maximum. Letter spacing is left unchanged.

With hyphenation turned off words are not allowed to break (hyphenate); this means that the text begins to develop unsightly and obvious gaps within the block. The third line is very loose, whilst the fifth line is very tight. The setting also creates a 'widow'.

In any given piece of text, hyphen-
ation and justification settings alter the overall appearance or 'colour' of the copy block. Word spacing, letter spacing and hyphenation settings all contribute to how a piece of text will appear.

The paragraph above is set with the same word spacing characteristics but is now allowed to hyphenate.

The inclusion of hyphens improves the appearance of the text block, but unsightly gaps still remain in the fifth line.

In any given piece of text, hyphen-
ation and justification settings alter the overall appearance or 'colour' of the copy block. Word spacing, letter spacing and hyphenation settings all contribute to how a piece of text will appear.

The paragraph above has justification values of 85% minimum, 100% optimum and 125% maximum. Letter spacing is allowed to alter by -5% to +5%.

The justification limits are narrower but have sufficient range to allow comfortable text spacing that looks neater, even though more hyphens are required. Gentle use of letter spacing helps to achieve this result.

In the final example (facing page) word and letter spacing are altered to enable the text to be set satisfactorily. Even though most computer programs will do this, it is worth considering exactly what is being changed. These values affect not only the setting of the text in a column but also the overall appearance of the text. Typefaces that are allowed to be tightly set will appear collapsed and text set too wide will look both ugly and unnecessarily hard to read.

The value of automatic hyphenation and justification is to assist the setting of large bodies of text. If only a small amount of the text is to be set, then this can of course be done manually.

Below is a brief synopsis of the visual impact when word and letter spacing values are altered.

altering word spacing

Word spacing, as the name implies, affects the spaces between words.

altering word spacing

Increasing word spacing proportionally increases the width of these spaces.

loose spacing

normal spacing

tight spacing

Letter spacing alters the spacing between individual characters. There are essentially three values described – loose, normal and tight – although in practice any value can be specified.

Word spacing

The distance between words (word spacing) can be increased or decreased whilst leaving the words unaltered.

Increasing word spacing will result in a 'whiter' body of text; conversely decreasing it will result in a more solid or 'grey' appearance.

Letter spacing

Increasing or decreasing the distance between the letters of a word (letter spacing) affects the appearance of the word, as it controls the extent to which one letter is allowed to occupy the space of another letter.

Hierarchy

The text hierarchy is a logical, organised and visual guide for the headings that accompany body text. It denotes varying levels of importance through point size and/or style.

The A head is the heading normally used for the title of a piece. It generally uses the largest point size or greatest weight to indicate its predominance, demonstrated here by use of bold type.

The second classification, the B head, normally has a smaller point size or lighter weight than an A head, although it remains larger and heavier than body text. B heads normally incorporate chapter headings. Here it is shown underlined.

Of the three standard heading categories specified, the C head is the lowest. It may be the same point size as the body text but could be an italic version of the font, as it is here.

Body copy is the main text block that follows a heading. In this hierarchy, it is separated from the C head by an empty line to introduce spacing and emphasise hierarchy.

Client: International School of Basel

Design: Form Design

Layout synopsis: Simple hierarchy using highlighting

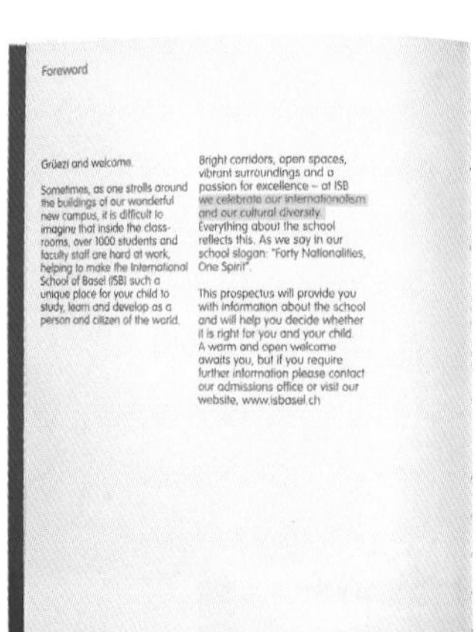

Foreword

Grüezi and welcome.

Sometimes, as one strolls around the buildings of our wonderful new campus, it is difficult to imagine that inside the classrooms, over 1000 students and faculty staff are hard at work, helping to make the International School of Basel (ISB) such a unique place for your child to study, learn and develop as a person and citizen of the world.

Bright corridors, open spaces, vibrant surroundings and a passion for excellence – at ISB we celebrate our internationalism and our cultural diversity. Everything about the school reflects this. As we say in our school slogan: "Forty Nationalities, One Spirit".

This prospectus will provide you with information about the school and will help you decide whether it is right for you and your child. A warm and open welcome awaits you, but if you require further information please contact our admissions office or visit our website, www.isbasel.ch

Introduction by
Peter J McMurray, Director

Mark Twain once wrote "travel is fatal to prejudice, bigotry, and narrow-mindedness... broad, wholesome, charitable views of men and things cannot be acquired by vegetating in one corner of the earth all one's lifetime". Although written more than 100 years ago, what he said then is even more relevant today.

At our school we are "Forty Nationalities, One Spirit"; you could say these are 'four words that sum up our belief', because at the ISB we aim to teach students how to be global citizens by celebrating the diversity that exists here.

Alongside the pursuit of excellence and personal fulfilment, we encourage students to be tolerant and understanding of different nationalities and cultures in an environment of mutual trust and respect. English is the language used in classes but we also offer German and French and a full curriculum including the Sciences, Physical Education, Literature, Information Technology and Food Technology.

As a school, we are delighted to report that ISB continues to grow and build on its success. Our most recent landmark took place on 26th August 2002 when the school completed its move to the new building in Reinach – a facility boasting outstanding resources and which promises to create exciting opportunities in the future.

We are firmly on the way to establishing ourselves as one of Europe's leading international schools. There has never been a more exciting time in the school's history and we hope that this prospectus will convey some of that dynamism.

If you like what you see, I would like to invite you to visit our campus to experience our work and our spirit.

International School of Basel

This prospectus for the International School of Basel uses a simple hierarchy. The box cover carries only a title, set in a rounded sans serif font and in warm colours that visually reinforce the subject matter: a Swiss brochure set in Swiss type style.

Internally distinct yellow backgrounds highlight the text and guide the reader to key information. Helping to structure the text information, these underpinning blocks of colour act as visual 'pointers' through a clean and restrained design.

Client: Booth-Clibborn Editions
Design: Why Not Associates
Layout synopsis: Clean, spacious, juxtaposed text blocks

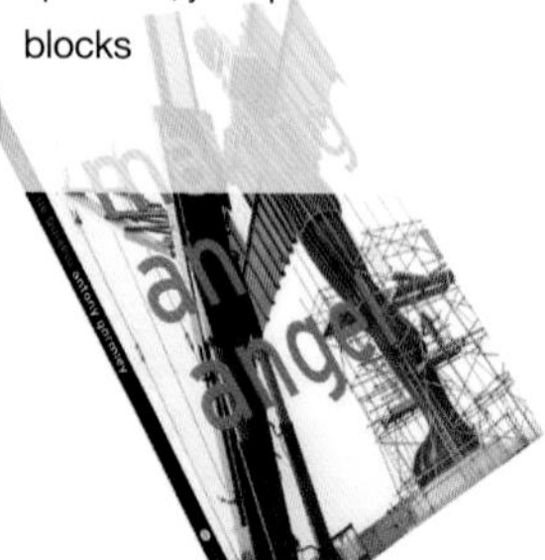

STEELWORK HEIGHT 20m
WINGSPAN 54m
WING HEIGHT AT BODY JUNCTION 6.2m
TOTAL WEIGHT 208 TONS
(EACH WING 50 TONS, BODY 108 TONS)
ANKLE CROSS-SECTION 780mm BY 1,400mm
(EQUIVALENT TO AN ORDINARY DOOR IN THE HOUSE)
3,153 PIECES OF STEEL ASSEMBLED
136 BOLTS NEEDED TO ATTACH WINGS TO BODY
(EACH 48mm DIAMETER)
22,000 MAN HOURS SPENT IN FABRICATION
(TWENTY MEN WORKING FULL-TIME FOR SIX MONTHS)
10km OF WELDING IN FABRICATION

DESIGN HORIZONTAL WIND FORCE ON WINGS 70 TONS
(EQUIVALENT TO THE ANGEL BOLTED TO A VERTICAL SURFACE
AND A 35-TON LORRY PARKED ON EACH WING)
450 TONS FORCE IN WING DIAPHRAGMS
1,200 TONS FORCE IN ANKLE RIBS
50 TONS FORCE IN EACH 50mm BOLT
(SO EACH BOLT COULD CARRY A LORRY AND A HALF)
2,500 MAN HOURS SPENT IN ENGINEERING DESIGN AND DRAWING
FOUNDATIONS **5000m³ OF SOIL EXCAVATED**
AND LATER REPLACED TO REFORM MOUND
100 TONS OF GROUT PUMPED INTO MINE WORKINGS
UP TO 33m BELOW GROUND
700 TONS OF CONCRETE AND 32 TONS OF REINFORCING STEEL
USED IN FOUNDATION EXTENDING 20m BELOW GROUND
52 BOLTS NEEDED TO HOLD ANGEL UPRIGHT IN WIND
(EACH 50mm DIAMETER AND 3m LONG)

an
enlightened
icarus
dr
stephanie
brown

making
an
angel

antony
gormley
gateshead
council

Making an Angel

This book, designed for Booth-Clibborn Editions by Why Not Associates, documents the creation of Antony Gormley's sculpture *The Angel of the North*.

The cover's spine text (top left) reads top to bottom and bottom to top, which means that when the book is placed on a table, half of it will be correct for reading.

A very distinctive typographical hierarchy is used, which utilises a variety of both point sizes and colours to make a visual feature of the titles.

Client: The Centre for Drawing
Design: Gavin Ambrose
Layout synopsis: Simple text and image positioning

What is Drawing?

This book designed for The Centre for Drawing features the work of artists Lucy Gunning, Claude Heath and Rae Smith. The book opens with a question mark and ends with a full stop – typographic icons that reflect the questioning nature of art and the conclusion of the book. A mixture of full-bleed images and tight, constrained grids often containing multiple sequential images (bottom left) varies the pace of the publication. Folio numbers sit on the right-hand side of every page edge so as you thumb through the publication you see the title of the book and one of the folio numbers because what is in the middle of the page disappears in the fold (see page 79).

Type style

The type style selected for a design plays a major part in establishing the character and mood of the piece. It can be aggressive, friendly, authorative or playful. In this spread, the curvaceous nature of the characters conveys a sense of creativity and are not overly authoritarian.

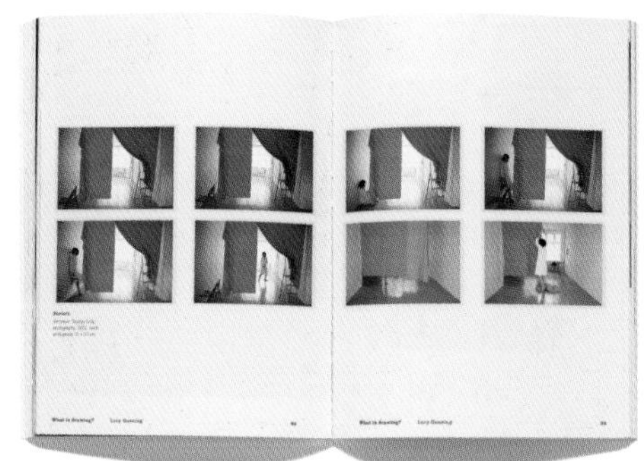

WHEN YOU FOLLOW THE MOVEMENTS OF A FOOTBALL ACROSS A FLAT TV SCREEN YOU SOMETIMES HAVE THE SENSATION THAT THE BALL IS GOING IN A CERTAIN DIRECTION WHEN IT TURNS OUT TO HAVE A DIFFERENT ARC ALTOGETHER AND ENDS UP AT THE FEET OF A DIFFERENT PLAYER THAN YOU HAD FIRST THOUGHT. ITS TRUE MOVEMENTS ARE HIDDEN BY THE FLATNESS OF THE SCREEN UNTIL IT ARRIVES AT SOME PARTICULAR PART OF THE PITCH. THIS SAME KIND OF SENSATION SOMETIMES HAPPENS WHILE DRAWING, WHEN YOU ATTEMPT TO COMPRESS THE SIGHT AND TOUCH OF A SOLID OBJECT ONTO VARIOUS PARTS OF A FLAT SURFACE. I WANT TO LOOK FURTHER INTO THIS.

WORKING FROM PLANTS NOW, IT WILL ALSO BE INTERESTING TO SEE WHETHER IT IS POSSIBLE TO SET THEM DOWN JUST AS THEY ARE, BUT AS IF RENDERED BY A THREE-DIMENSIONAL COMPUTER PROGRAMME THAT HAS TAKEN A HOLIDAY FROM MATHEMATICS.

Claude Heath, October 2001

What is drawing? Claude Heath 97

Claude Heath was born in London in 1964 and studied Philosophy at King's College, London (1983-1986). He lives and works in London.

He had his first solo exhibition in London in 1995 at Hales Gallery. In 1996 he was included in *Young British Artists VI* at the Saatchi Gallery, London and *The Whitechapel Open* at Whitechapel Art Gallery, London. More recently, he has exhibited at De Appel Foundation, Amsterdam and in *The John Moores Exhibition 20* (as a prize-winner), Walker Art Gallery, Liverpool, 1997; in *The Whitechapel Open* and in *Antechamber* at the Whitechapel Art Gallery, London and in *The Jerwood Painting Prize* at the Jerwood Space, London, 1998; in *The John Moores Exhibition 21*, Walker Art Gallery, Liverpool, in *The Natwest Art Prize*, at Lothbury, London, at Nicole Klagsbrun Gallery, New York, and at the Henry Moore Institute/ Leeds City Art Gallery, 1999; in *Art in Sacred Spaces*, a Millenium Fund commission and school residency at Christchurch, Isle of Dogs, London, 2000; at Paul Kasmin Gallery, New York, at the British Museum, London, and at Essor Gallery, London, 2001; and at Kettle's Yard Gallery, Cambridge, 2002.

Heath was the first artist in residence at the Henry Moore Institute and this led to his solo exhibition at Leeds City Art Gallery. He is the 2002-2003 Kettle's Yard Artist Fellow at Christ's College, Cambridge.

His work is included in a number of collections, including the Arts Council Collection at the Hayward Gallery, The British Museum, Deutsche Bank, the Henry Moore Institute and the Walker Art Gallery.

Claude Heath is represented by Paul Kasmin Gallery, New York.

Rae Smith: What drawing feels like

Having collaborated with Rae Smith on seven pieces of work for the theatre, I am used to encountering her drawings as part of the working process of putting on a show. When we collaborate (she designs, I direct) drawings are the most effective means of summarising or explaining our ideas for the realisation of the piece, both to each other and to other people. These theatre drawings, though they are often (or indeed usually) incidentally beautiful, are drawings of a particular kind; explanatory, illustrative and disposable. The drawings published here are something different; they were, for instance, made in private, not in collaboration, and they were meant for exhibition.

Because of its usual scale, and its traditional materials, and because it is so intimately to do with the workings of the hand, drawing comes closest to handwriting in the index of forms of expression. A drawing is often almost an unintentional autograph, a signature. Sometimes Smith delights in this aspect of drawing quite directly, with rapidly executed ink sketches that are torn out of a notepaper-sized sketchbook and simply 'Blu-tacked' to the wall – memos. Even when the drawings are blown up to an unframable scale, and made directly onto the wall, they still carefully retain their hand-drawn-ness. They are still clearly 'pages' from a notebook. In addition, the pages seem to be from something as near to a journal as to a sketchbook. Traditionally, the sketchbook accompanies the artist and is used to quickly record impressions while she is outside, travelling, impressions which she will then work up into something else in the privacy of her studio. In this case, not just the working-up but the journeys themselves have been made within the locked room of the studio. They are all journeys into memory or enquiry – especially memory. There are no life-drawings or *plein air* landscape sketches here. These figures and landscapes are all remembered, seen with the mind's eyes. What is remembered is then recorded, reworked and recontextualised within an elaborate and self-reflexive notion of what a 'simple' thing a drawing is.

The room that Smith has made takes the idea of an exhibition of drawings, and turns it into a small theatrical event – an event for an audience of one (on reflection, that probably makes it an installation; however, I strongly suspect that she wants the viewer to 'perform', and be aware of performing, the act of looking at her drawings, so I'll stick with the notion of theatricality – after all, there is atmospheric and technically contrived lighting, every surface is treated and dramatised, there is a soundtrack, programme notes, a clear sequence of events, an expressive climax in the final drawing before the end...). The room in which she has installed the work has been worked and manipulated so that each drawing is a contributory part of an overall experience of the space itself, and of the time that the individual viewer spends within it. In this respect, I think that her model (subconscious or conscious) is not the obvious one of a white-painted art gallery, but rather a tiny whitewashed mediaeval chapel – somewhere like the one at Coombes in East Sussex which we visited together in the winter of 2001. The walls of this intensely atmospheric space are covered in sporadically visible traces of all-over eleventh-century wall paintings of extraordinary vigour and delicacy. The paintings – or wall-drawings – are so decayed that you need to look very hard to see what they are of, and even where they are; even so, the viewer is aware that all the fragments are part of a larger scheme. Smith has made the accidental effects of this painted chapel deliberate. In her room also, none of the drawings are in black and white, or framed, or easily visible. They are too big, too small, spread across architectural features, too high, too low, too detailed, too incomplete. Even when they are perfectly preserved and legible, they are in eye-exercising fluorescent ink, or in evocative white-on-white. The viewer must work, quite literally, to see them, and in consequence, to feel them. However, they never intend to frustrate; they always work to encourage concentration, and resonance. The effect, as in the chapel, is as emotive as it is pleasurable.

As in a mediaeval church, drawing here has several both distinct and overlapping functions – it is by turns mnemonic, educative, iconographic, narrative, devotional and decorative. This is in part an effect of summarising the various fruits of an intensive period of full-time studio work. Smith is quite unapologetic about refusing to limit 'drawing' to one particular or privileged function. The drawings of men storytelling or playing music are terrific celebrations of a personal taste for virile energy; drawing as manifest enthusiasm. *Dream* is an evocation of a mood, a storyboarded urban landscape which houses a fantasia on freedom; drawing as contemporary pastoral, escaping from two dimensions just as the mind escapes the city. Pieces like *Door* or *Dragonfly* unashamedly use drawing to work something out – they are sketches of ideas, quite literally. If importance is to be measured by intensity of feeling, then the two most important drawings in the room are *Scissors* and *Medja*. Several kinds of drawing are here combined to complex effect. An apparently random stack of pages torn from a sketchpad allude to the traditional sketchbook attempts to fix an image before transferring it to canvas, but in fact the repetition here re-enacts the compulsive re-viewing of a horrific and unwanted memory.

What is drawing? Rae Smith: What drawing feels like 119

A simple typographic hierarchy is used to separate distinct sections of the book. Pictured clockwise (from top left): the artist's statement page using condensed News Gothic opposite a full-bleed image; centred full stop; an essay spread using Clarendon ranged left and two text columns; and a biography page using bold Clarendon in a single text column opposite a full-bleed image of the artist.

The typographical hierarchy uses a large point size to make titles a key visual feature, which fits with the use of punctuation as images.

Arrangement

The different elements that will comprise a design, predominantly the type and images, could be treated as separate components that are to be arranged on the page with clear distinctions between them.

Alternatively, they can be combined to form a seamless presentation. This can be achieved in many different ways as the examples that follow will show.

Combining images and text can be used as a method to control the pace of a publication. Publications often have clear and natural break points such as new chapters. However, seemingly unrelated information can be brought together in a cohesive manner through design.

The Stones 65–67 (right)

This book by British photographer Gered Mankowitz, designed by Spin, uses a four-column grid and oversized imagery that retains the original reportage style of the images. With attention clearly focused on the photographs, the typography is understated and set closely.

Type and image are treated and arranged as separate elements but the consistent approach unifies these elements into a coherent whole. The opening, type-free section prints in duotone on an uncoated stock and the main body of the book prints on a satin stock.

Client: Vision On

Design: Spin

Layout synopsis: Separation of type and image

Reportage photography captures hidden and defining moments of people or events that are both factual and full of humanity.

Client: MTV

Design: Form Design

Layout synopsis: Unstructured, energetic, assimilated scrapbook-style pages

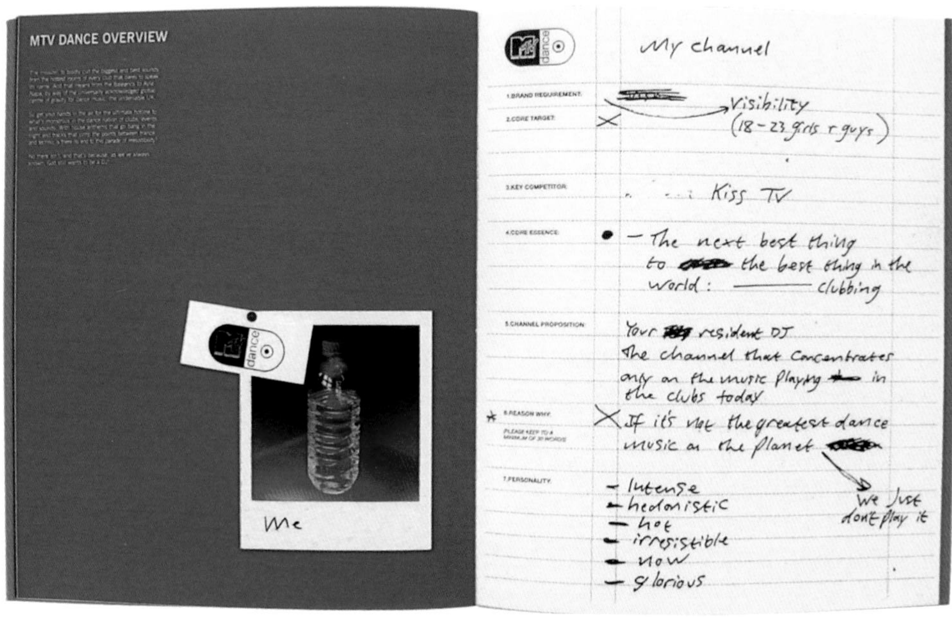

MTV (left)

This digital channel brand manual for MTV created by Form Design features type and images that link to form a larger overall picture. The formal constraints are removed by the use of handwritten type, which adds a dynamic element to the design. The energy of MTV is captured through the layout and typography and the designers successfully managed to avoid creating a staid and stifled corporate document.

George & Vera (right)

This self-promotional publication by George & Vera has a very structured layout underpinned by a module-based grid (bottom). Each field replicates the same graphic (centre) which is then overprinted on top of the text. The grid is also used to position marginalia and body text on photograph-dominated spreads (top).

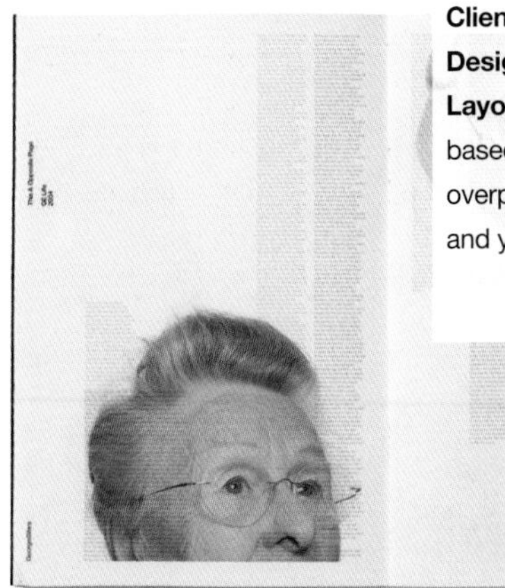

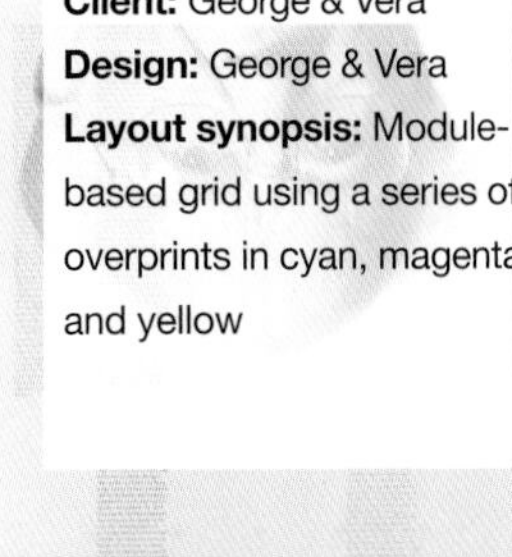

Client: George & Vera
Design: George & Vera
Layout synopsis: Module-based grid using a series of overprints in cyan, magenta and yellow

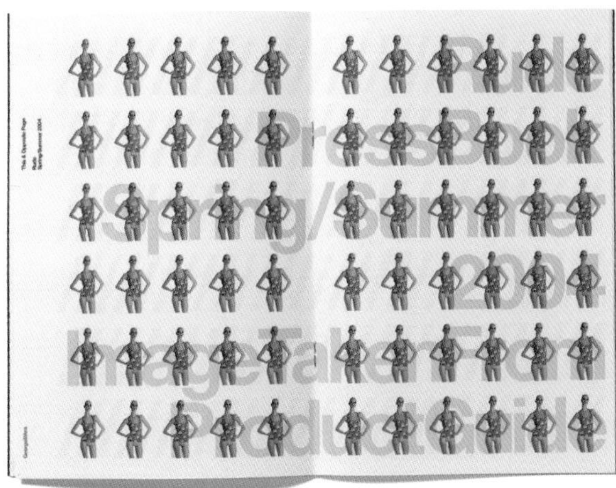

Client: Violette Editions
Design: Aboud Sodano
Layout synopsis: Format constrained, passe partout image presentation

Form and Function

The form that a layout of a work takes is driven by the function of the design, the ideas and information it has to communicate, the medium in which this will occur and the target audience.

Whilst fundamental layout principles can be used to achieve a high degree of creativity, their basic purpose is functional, to achieve a well-balanced design that presents the various page elements clearly.

'Simplicity before understanding is simplistic; simplicity after understanding is simple.'
Edward De Bono

Father + Son (left)

This small format book by Aboud Sodano for Violette Editions is essentially two books conjoined. The left-hand book is a collection of photographs by Harold Smith and the right-hand book is a collection of Paul Smith's images.

The design means both books can be viewed simultaneously allowing the spreads to become a juxtaposition of photographic styles and eras. Harold's images are nearly all black and white and are reproduced with a sepia tone. Paul's are far brighter, with an almost Loma (highly saturated colour) quality to them.

The passe partout layout is constrained by the small format of the work and presentation of nearly full-page photographs.

Dividing the book

Client: CCAC Wattis Institute
Design: Aufuldish + Warinner
Layout synopsis: Book divided into two halves, each with front cover

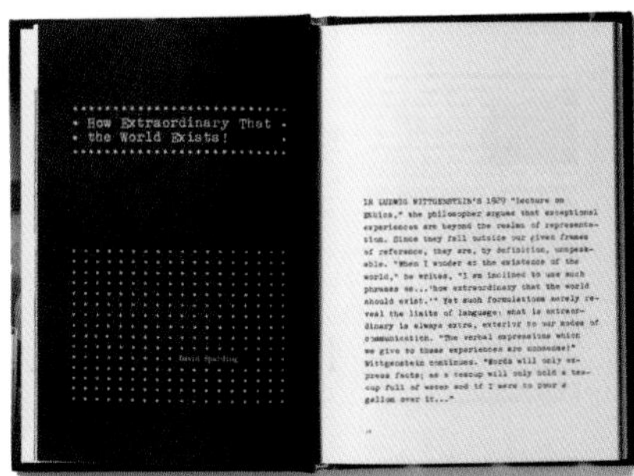

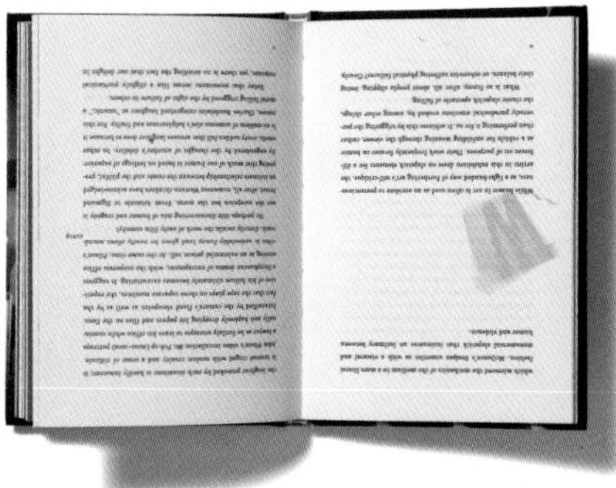

Sudden Glory **How Extraordinary that the World Exists!**

These two exhibition catalogues for the CCAC Wattis Institute are contained within one book. The design by Aufuldish + Warinner divides the publication into two parts; one for each exhibition. The covers serve as individual front covers for both parts and flipping the book over presents the start of each. This is a simple, effective and neat way of dividing the two distinct elements that the publication contains.

The magenta spread (middle row, right) is the point where both catalogues join. The three spreads shown on the top and middle rows are from *How Extraordinary that the World Exists!* and the remaining spreads are from *Sudden Glory*.

Client: Becks Futures
Design: Research Studios
Layout synopsis: Vertical running text to elongate a page

Becks Futures

This horizontal A4 brochure for the Becks Futures 2004 art prize designed by Research Studios contains a series of essays that are saddle-stitched into an A3 brochure containing images by the shortlisted artists. Text in the oversize brochure (right) runs vertically whilst text in the outer brochure runs horizontally. The vertical text further elongates the page of the oversize part.

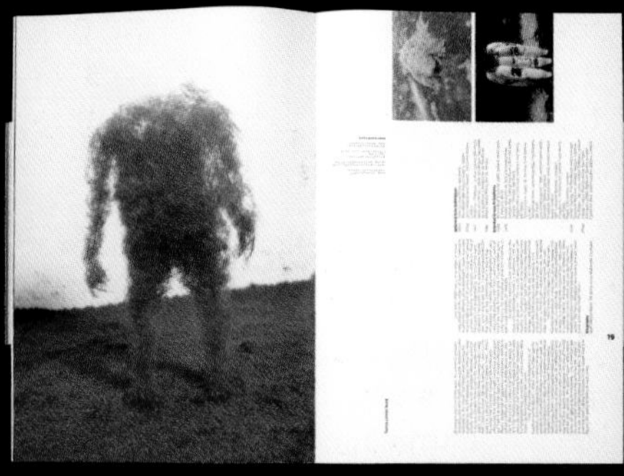

Client: Forth Estate
Design: Research Studios
Layout synopsis: Divides entries into text and images

Forth Estate

This catalogue for Forth Estate publications by Research Studios is bound, folded and trimmed into two distinct sections. Sixteen pages are printed on uncoated paper and 16 are printed on a gloss stock. When folded, the publication gives the appearance of two different books bound together. For each entry, an abstracted image appears in the front section with accompanying text printed in the larger back section.

Format plays a major role in the appearance of this work. Layout, and the placement of text and images, is used to make the publication look like an artist's sketchbook at the beginning where the images are placed, and a traditional book towards the end where the text is.

St Philip's Church, Stratford Road (following pages)

The front section of this book by North design studio for the property developing Manhattan Loft Corporation repeatedly uses passe partout to lay out portraits by Amber Rowlands. This framing provides commonality and helps maintain the religious theme insofar as they all look like a common image of Jesus Christ.

The text section that follows uses a classic asymmetrical layout; the two text blocks are shunted left with a wide right-hand margin. The front section is printed on a Chromolux paper, which is high gloss one side and uncoated the other. The back section is on a light grey pulp stock.

Client: Manhattan Loft Corporation
Design: North
Layout synopsis: Passe partout provides consistent image presentation, asymmetrical grid for text

Westbourne Grove, Notting Hill, London. W11
Within today's city a district can often be seen
striving for a sense of community, an intangible feeling
which can set the area apart from its surroundings.
Notting Hill has truly achieved this spirit, having
been the focus for a vibrant and bohemian community
since the 1950's. For a decade or so the area has been
the centre of a great property boom, built on a sense
of the past but informed by a firm grasp of the future.
These factors have helped to build a neighbourhood
which actively encourages individuality. This is most
visible on the stalls of Portobello Road market, where
antiques and fresh produce from around the world are
sold alongside vintage clothing and furniture straight
from the pages of Vogue.
Move away from the bustle of the market and onto the
side streets and many of the capital's most sought
after interior design and fashion boutiques can be
found, including The Cross, Matches, Solange Azagury-
Partridge, Themes and Variations and Christopher Farr.
Several established retailers are also in Notting Hill,
among them Paul & Joe and Paul Smith, whose wonderfully
eclectic Westbourne House is a new addition to the
excellent shopping to be found in the area. The many
new stores on and around Westbourne Grove have made
the area something of a focus for London's young design
talent, and these new boutiques sit comfortably next
to the antique and collectible shops for which the
area is rightly famous.
Westbourne Grove lies at the centre of Notting Hill
and it is here at the junction of Ledbury Road that
Westbourne Grove Church is situat
location for living in Notting
area truly comes to life, a weal
as E&O are only minutes away.
celebrated pubs The Westbourne an
Cow are located within walking dis
bars and eateries. From this location,
understand the draw of Notting Hill and
holds for many of London's young
Loft Corporation has sought to develop the
Grove Church with the surrounding area in
building has been altered radically; to
today's property needs, two new floors and a
car park have been added, ensuring secure
parking for every apartment. The character
church will still remain in features such as
rose windows in all the third floor
the unique circular rooms defined by the
church towers and the original church
of which will be retained on the ground and
floors.
apartments (of which seven are duplexes)
sold as shells, giving the buyer the ultimate
to express his or her individuality. After
the shells in a fully serviced state – all
services, telephone, broadband, cable and satellite
connections ready – the possibilities for
interiors of the apartments are limitless.
development of Westbourne Grove Church and subsequent
transformation of the apartments within, will add an
exciting and unique dimension to what is understandably
one of London's prime residential areas. The apartments
are being sold with the benefit of 125 year leases.

Appropriation

Client: Birkhäuser
Design: Studio Myerscough
Layout synopsis: Different stocks to divide publication

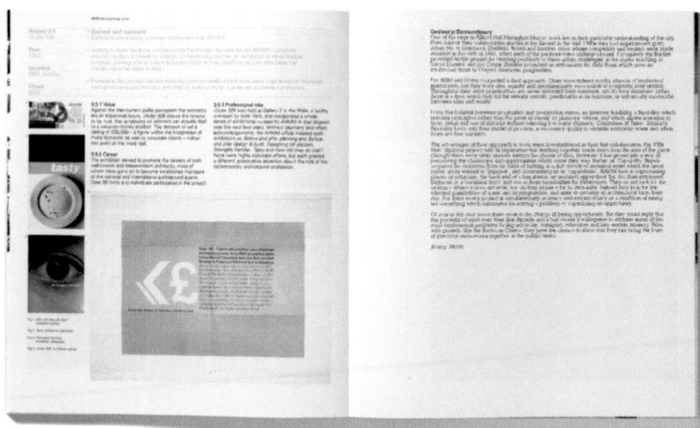

A variety of column widths, measures and image sizes create an eclectic scrapbook effect. The wide margin easily accommodates both images and captions. Solid magenta, cyan and black text separates the narrative into manageable blocks.

A series of rules separates information into related blocks. This simple device adds clarity and eases navigation when dealing with difficult tabular matter.

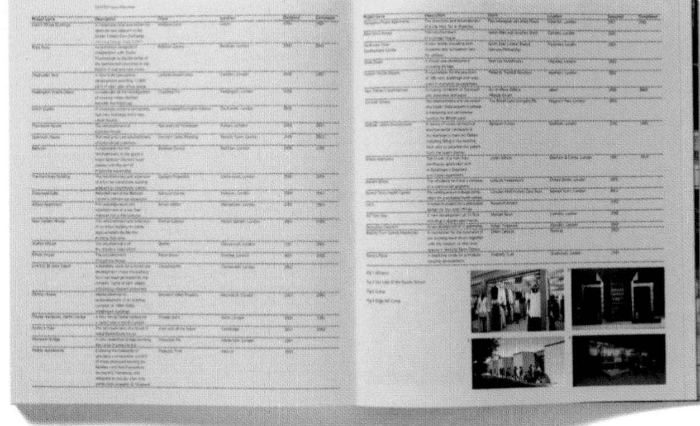

Manual – The Architecture and Office of Allford Hall Monaghan Morris

This book by Birkhäuser documents the work of contemporary architecture practice Allford Hall Monaghan Morris (AHMM). Studio Myerscough borrowed from the publication's name and designed the book specifically to resemble a manual. The back section is printed on an uncoated yellow paper stock that creates the impression of a glossary. The front section is printed on a silk stock. These stocks create two distinct areas for different information and impart texture to the publication.

Appropriation

Appropriation is the borrowing of a style, typically used elsewhere, as the basis for a design. This may be done for purely aesthetic reasons as a method to present information in a certain way, but often it is done to borrow characteristics that are associated with the appropriated source. Establishing such a connection may add credibility to the design or cause it to be viewed in a certain way. For example, presenting the content as if in a manual (as above) may mean the publication is perceived as being more authoritative.

Client: Forth Estate

Design: North

Layout synopsis: Revisiting conventions for a fresh approach

Thirst

This Nigel Slater cookbook by North design studio reinterprets traditional conventions to produce a fresh approach to a perennial problem; how to present a series of instructions without them appearing boring! The design uses a mixture of American typewriter fonts; ingredient lists and titles appear in light, and body copy is presented in bold. The text also has abstract images within its characters, which blends with the soft hues of Angela Moore's photographs.

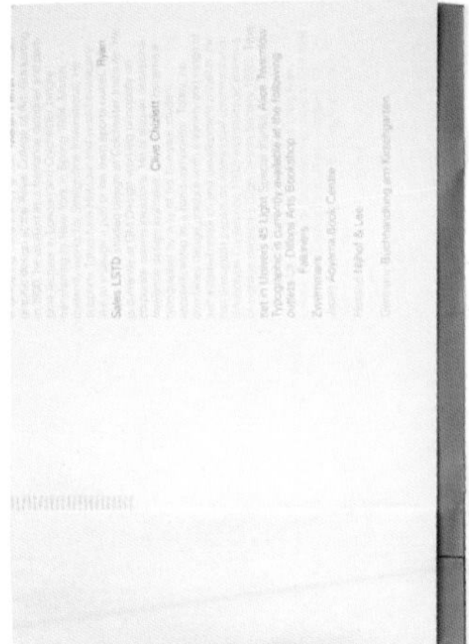

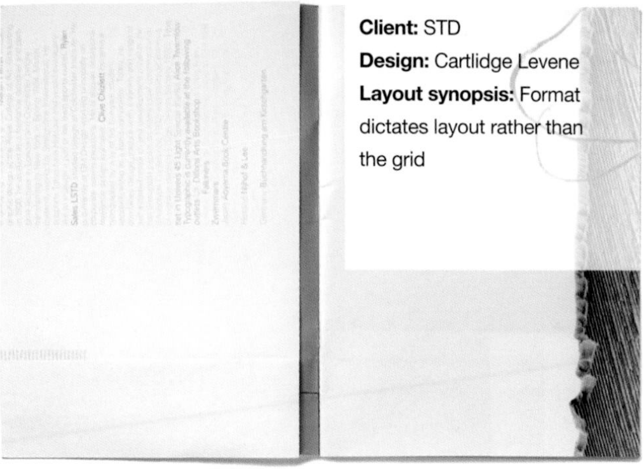

Client: STD
Design: Cartlidge Levene
Layout synopsis: Format dictates layout rather than the grid

STD

The Society of Typographic Designers (STD) uses a different design studio to create each issue of its journal. For this issue, design studio Cartlidge Levene used two double-sided posters that were cut, folded and trimmed to form the publication. In contrast to a typical publication design where space is divided by a grid, this format provides a degree of randomness to both the positioning of images and the hierarchy of information.

Exquisite corpse

The exquisite corpse (cadavre exquis) is a surrealist technique that exploits the happy chance of accident in the production of words or images.

The concept has a similar basis as the 'consequences' game whereby several people take turns to write or draw something on a piece of paper, then fold it to conceal what they have done before passing it on to the next person, who then repeats the actions.

This same technique is used by designers with the exception that the elements are deliberately selected or formed so that they will be compatible, as the example opposite shows.

Bodas (right)

Bodas, an underwear retailer, asked Rose Design to create the mail order catalogue that launched the company and proved to be a very successful marketing tool. Rose Design created a single-colour catalogue with centred cross-cut pages that formed an exquisite corpse so that readers are able to interact with the models and view different clothing combinations.

Client: Bodas

Design: Rose Design

Layout synopsis: Cross-cut pages provide exquisite corpse

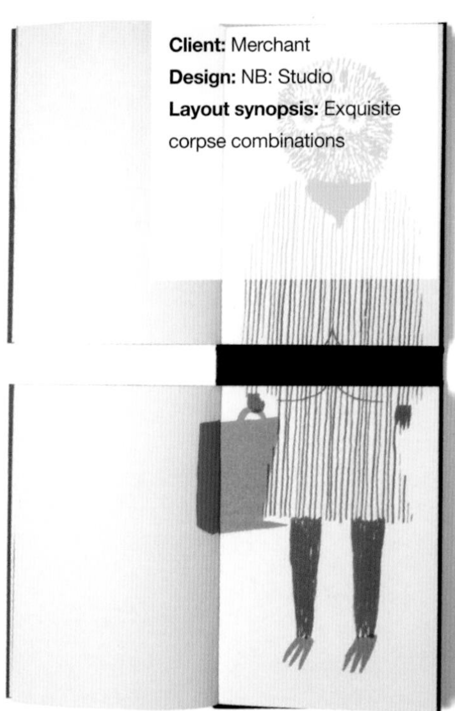

Client: Merchant
Design: NB: Studio
Layout synopsis: Exquisite corpse combinations

Two Minds

Merchant is an organisation that collaborates with design studios in the creation of annual reports. Together with NB: Studio they did something a little different for their own annual journal, which contains advice on design, current reporting trends and topical issues.

The journal comprises two 44-page books bound together into an embossed outer cover, which opens vertically so that each book can then be opened horizontally.

The split page throws up exquisite corpse combinations in sequence and, more interestingly, out of sequence.

Client: Staverton
Design: Form Design
Layout synopsis: Images of different sizes balanced with centred titles

Landscape™

Landscape

This brochure for furniture company Staverton by Form Design features a number of cropped images, some of which extend over the double-page spread to convey a feeling of space. This is mirrored in the landscape image used on the front cover.

Several of the spreads feature a series of sequential images showing the furniture in use. Titles are centred both horizontally and vertically, adding balance and importance to the brand's message.

Binding

Binding is a format choice that directly affects layout as the various binding methods (such as perfect binding, saddle-stitch and wiro binding) produce different physical attributes in the resulting product.

Perfect bound publications require a larger inner margin because the book will be pinched in at its spine when opened; while wiro bound publications should not have content in the central margin because it will be punctured by the physical binding process.

The Arts Foundation (right)

This brochure includes details of the designers, poets, documentary makers and performers shortlisted for the 2003 awards of The Arts Foundation in the UK.

The layout and the format are amorphous, seemingly without the shape or structure that can usually be seen at work in a design.

Images and text appear to be spontaneously positioned and the format comprises four odd-sized sheets that are folded, collated and bound with a plastic cable tie. In this way the design echoes the diverse areas for which the awards are given.

Using a cable tie as the binding method gives a unique touch to the piece and is a good fit with the assemblage approach. A more traditional binding would provide too much structure and diminish the anarchic feel obtained.

Client: The Arts Foundation
Design: Studio Myerscough
Layout synopsis: Four different-sized pages, collated and bound by a single plastic cable tie

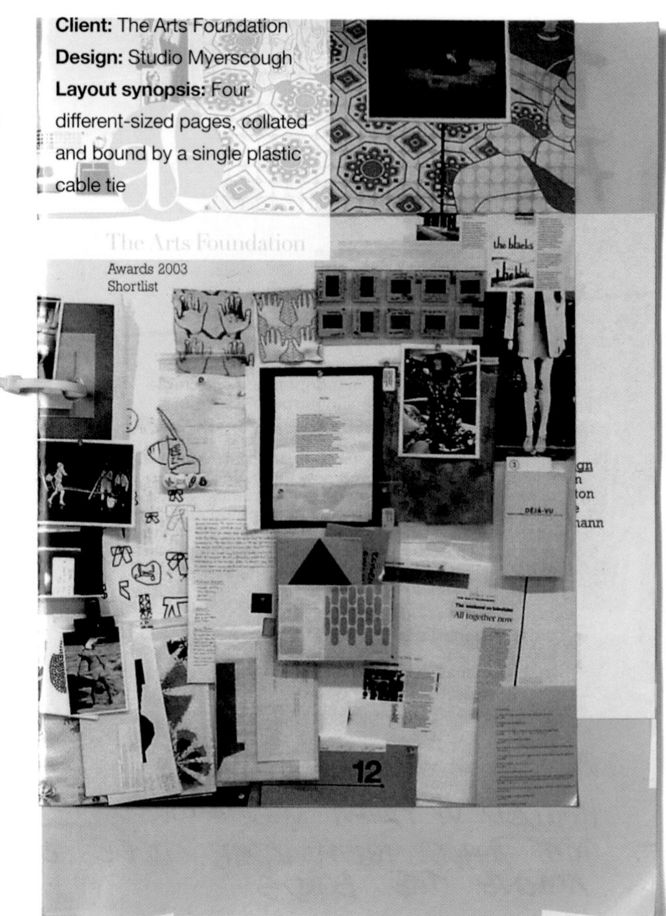

Assemblage

An assemblage is an artistic composition made from various odds and ends centred around a specific theme or, as in the example given, bringing together several different themes.

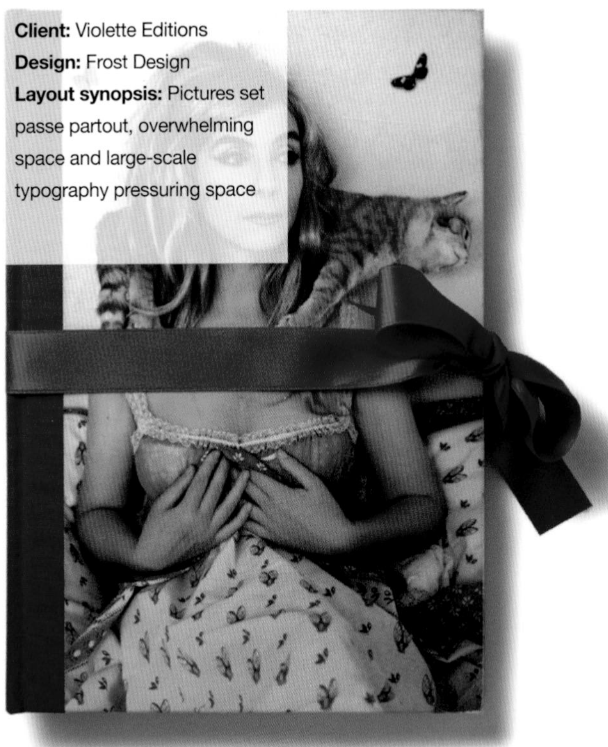

Client: Violette Editions

Design: Frost Design

Layout synopsis: Pictures set passe partout, overwhelming space and large-scale typography pressuring space

Double Game

This book design features images displayed passe partout, which are almost overwhelmed by the space that surrounds and faces them.

The gutter of the publication's binding is used to good effect to divide those spreads featuring book pages (below bottom right) but is ignored completely on others (below top right) as the text disappears into and emerges from it.

The use of large-scale typographical elements compounds the feeling of pressured space and is sympathetic to the New York setting of the work.

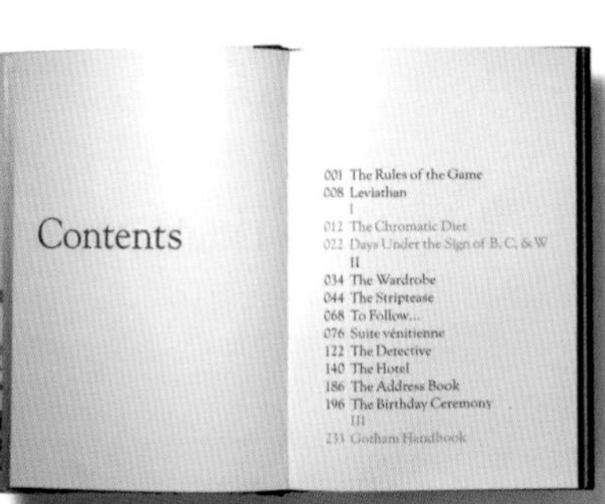

Client: Palau de la Virreina
Design: Bis
Layout synopsis: Flexible use of grid

Vostestaqui (You are here)

This catalogue is for a contemporary art exhibition in which the work of a number of different artists needed to be organised as a single unit. Bis design studio used a solid grid but one that had the flexibility to present the pages for different artists and expressed the individual artists' personality. The layout features simple colour blocks on single-leaf sheets with double binding holes in one margin. Text columns and picture widths are equal (centre).

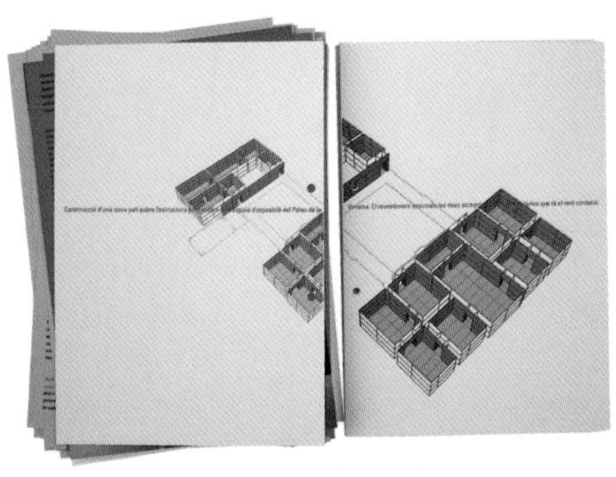

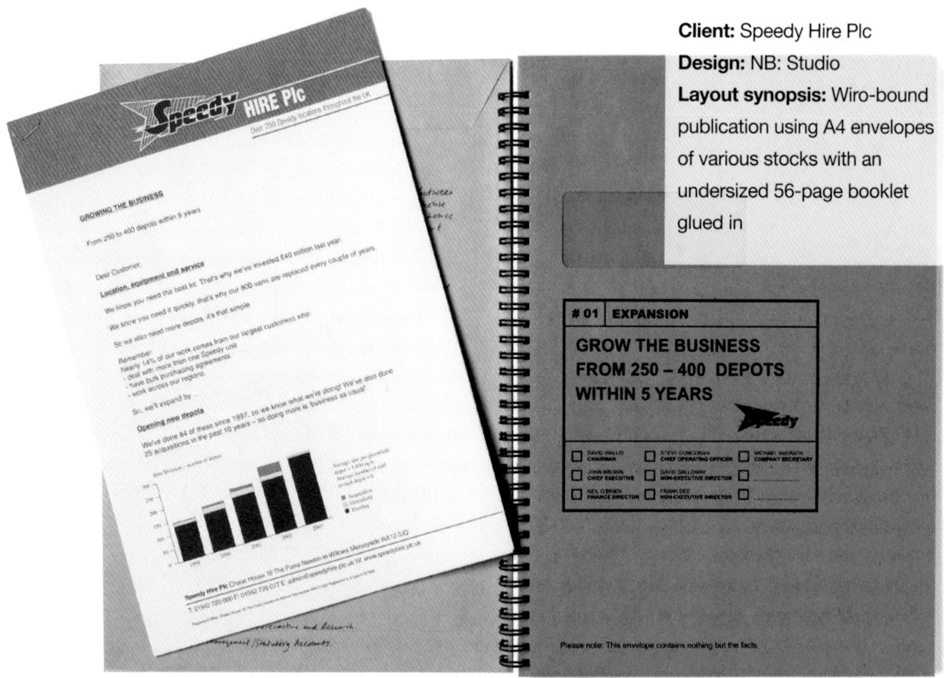

Client: Speedy Hire Plc
Design: NB: Studio
Layout synopsis: Wiro-bound publication using A4 envelopes of various stocks with an undersized 56-page booklet glued in

Speedy Hire Annual Report

When creating this design for the annual report of Speedy Hire Plc, NB: Studio cleaned out its stationery cupboard. The principal pages contain different stocks of A4 envelopes and a 56-page undersized booklet is glued into the back cover. The stationery theme is maintained as the report's pages are designed as letterheads, memos and other internal documentation.

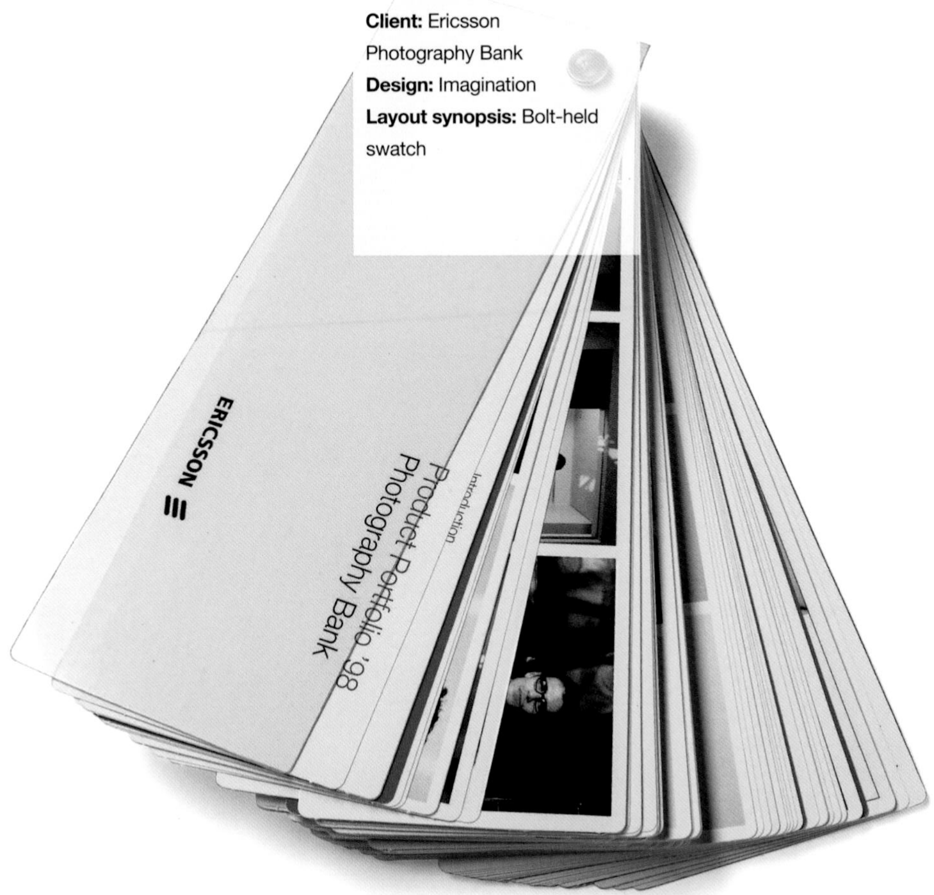

Client: Ericsson Photography Bank
Design: Imagination
Layout synopsis: Bolt-held swatch

Ericsson Photography Bank

Often the layout of a design is directly influenced by the format in which it is to be produced, as this example for the Ericsson Photography Bank shows.

As the publication was designed to be close at hand and easy to browse, Imagination chose to display the images in a swatch format. The unusual short and wide page dimensions clearly dictate the layout and the images appear as if in a film strip. As the swatch pages are held by a bolt in the corner the viewer can quickly scan through them.

Swatch

Typically a swatch is a bolt-held book of colour samples (also called a colour swatch) but may also contain material samples such as wallpaper, carpet or photographs, as shown in the example above.

Layout in Use

Client: Prestel
Design: Frost Design
Layout synopsis: Elongated format supporting the subject matter, complementary elongated layout

0:TEXAS 0040: APPALACHIA 0062: NORTHEAST

Layout in Use

A key function of layout is to let the elements, especially the image elements, perform the tasks that they have been selected for. Images add drama and emotion to a work, but how they communicate with the recipient depends upon how they are presented.

The following pages will provide examples of how layout choices in the presentation of images can be used to enhance or instill a certain feeling or attitude to the material.

'The rule: the fewer the differences in the size of the illustrations, the quieter the impression created by the design. As a controlling system the grid makes it easier to give the surface or space a rational organisation.'
Josef Müller-Brockmann

Some Trains in America (left)

For this book design for *Some Trains in America* by Andrew Cross, Frost Design used large, uninterrupted images where possible in the thin, horizontal format to frame the trains and capture a feeling of the open wilderness through which they are passing, thus celebrating the poignant beauty of the American landscape.

Scale

Scale, when used in design terminology, applies to the size of images and text. For the purpose of this volume we are looking at how big or small these elements are on the page. Choices here affect the weight with which we view an image.

An image with a large scale dominates the page and is the focus of attention, yet making a graphic too large can result in suffocation. At a smaller scale the information contained within the image may be missed or ignored.

Client: Gagosian Gallery
Design: North
Layout synopsis: Use of scale to show detail and full and complete pictures

Territories

This brochure was produced by North design studio to accompany a Jenny Saville exhibition at the New York Gagosian Gallery. Scale is a key feature of Saville's work and was used in the brochure to reproduce vivid details of her paintings.

A detail of *Fulcrum* (top) at 100% with a reproduction of the entire piece contained within a gatefold flap (middle).

Ruben's Flap (bottom) is 305cm x 244cm at 100%. Overleaf is a detail of this reproduced at 25% (verso) facing a detail of *Brace* shown at 50% (recto).

This use of scale allows the detail of the images to be clearly viewed and this adds credibility to the catalogue as a record of the work.

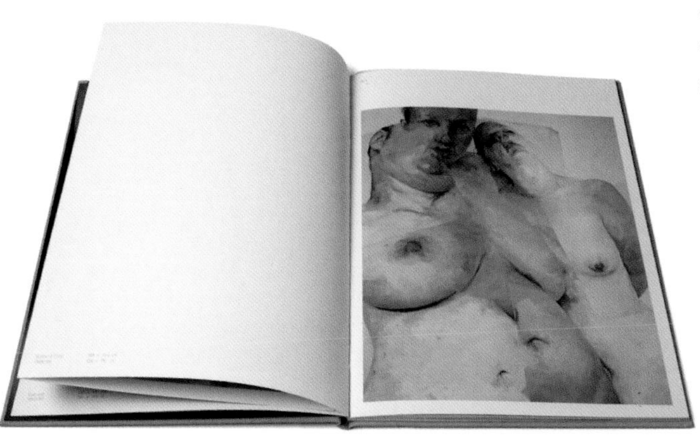

Ruben's Flap
1998/99

Detail at
25%

Ruben's Flap

This detail of *Ruben's Flap* is reproduced at 25% to provide a better sense of the scale of Saville's work. This faces a detail from *Brace*; these are two separate works.

Brace

This detail of *Brace* is reproduced at 50%.

Indexing

Many types of publication need to contain adjunct information whether displayed as a contents page, a formal index, a glossary of terms or a list of contact addresses.

Such varied types and quantities of information that require presentation can be quite challenging from a design point of view. As the following examples show, index pieces can be incorporated into the design in a number of ways that do not detract from the main body of the work.

Westzone – New Angles on Life (right)

This catalogue layout for Westzone Publishing by Rose Design has the publication titles and author names printed on the inside front and back flaps. A silver panel contains each book's specification information. An arrow on every page points to the author in the silver panel and links them to the iconic image reproduced in the catalogue.

In order to develop the overall brand, images displayed in the catalogue feature the word 'Westzone'. On the flag it appears as a screen print, under the hat it is found as a footnote, on the image of the doll it's a glint in the eye and it is seen as a manufacturing mark on the model kit.

Client: Westzone Publishing
Design: Rose Design
Layout synopsis: Author details on front strip with arrow identification system

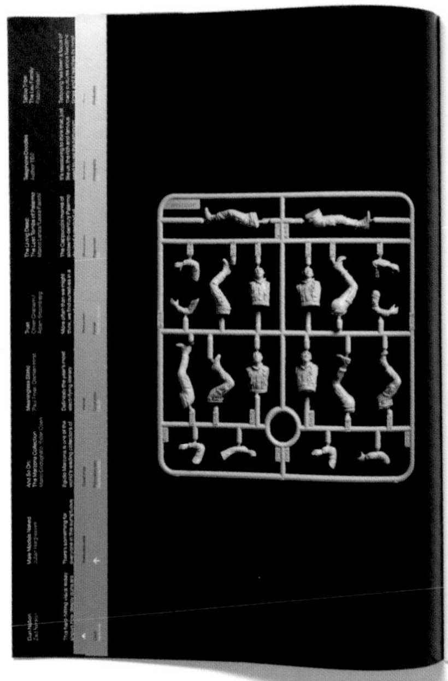

Client: Vision On
Design: SEA Design
Layout synopsis: Photograph placed to wraparound cut edge

Rankin Nudes

This book of nudes by London-based fashion photographer Rankin was created by SEA Design for publisher Vision On. It is common for cover images to wraparound the spine, but this picture of fashion model Kate Moss is wrapped around the cute edge. The placement of the picture here provides a double take as her eye appears in the slither of the inside back cover.

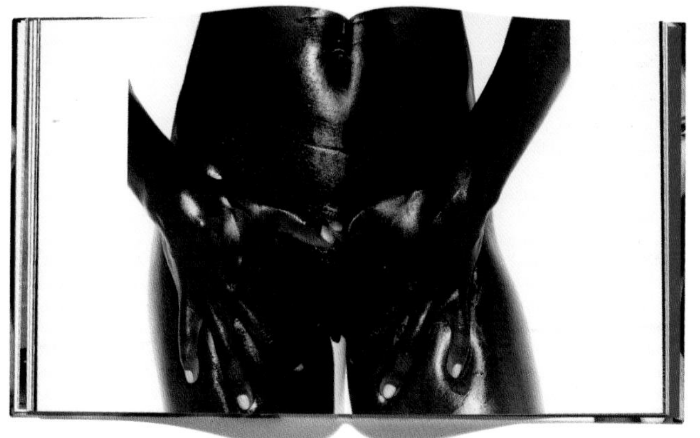

Preserving the essence
Rankin is one of the world's leading contemporary fashion photographers with a style that can be blunt, stark and confrontational. SEA Design studio preserved this by combining image placement with the provocative use of the central gutter in this glorious and unashamed reproduction.

Pictures not words
With images that speak for themselves typography was kept to a minimum and given low-key treatment as this half-title page shows.

Thumbnail index
SEA provided a monotone-thumbnail index detailing who the sitters were in order to leave the spreads free from typographic intervention, allowing the viewer to focus solely on the images. The index typography is subtle and passive giving dominance to the thumbnail photographs.

Orientation

Orientation refers to the plane or direction in which the elements of a design are used. Text and images are typically set so that they are read and viewed horizontally from left to right. Using other orientations such as vertical or angled is done typically to maintain a particular aesthetic in the design, as doing so makes the reader work harder to obtain the information by having to rotate the publication. This may encourage them to pay more attention to it, but can also have an adverse effect and make them lose interest.

Dialogue (right)

Dialogue contains a selection of thoughts and ideas from the architectural practice Central Workshop. Design studio Thirteen changed the orientation of each spread so that the reader has to rotate the publication at every turn of the page. New ideas may involve radical departures from commonly accepted practices and these ideas are presented in such a way that the reader is required to challenge accepted norms for using a book. The square format eases this reorientation as the guides essentially remain in the same place.

Client: Central Workshop

Design: Thirteen

Layout synopsis: Rotating orientation in square format

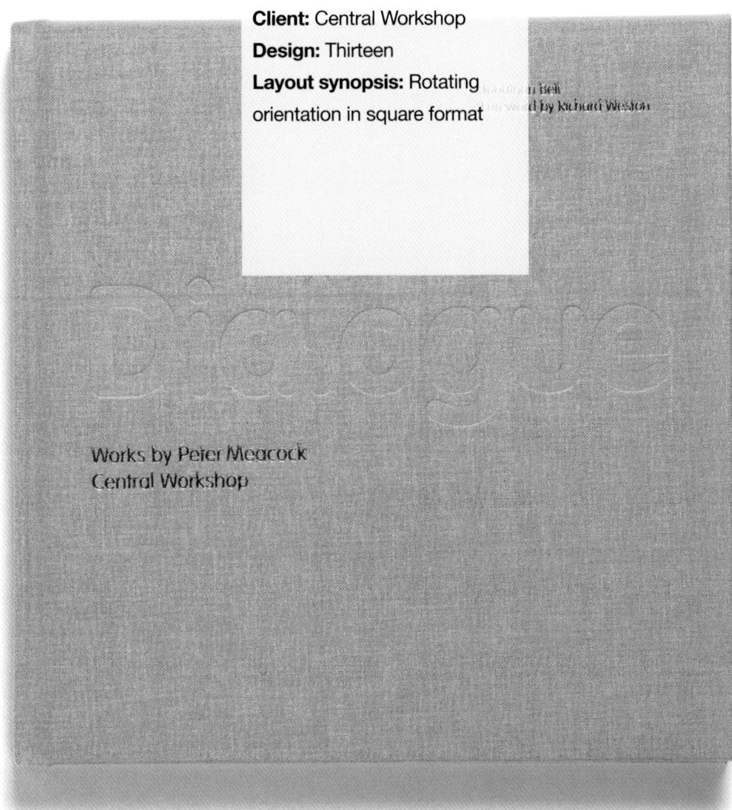

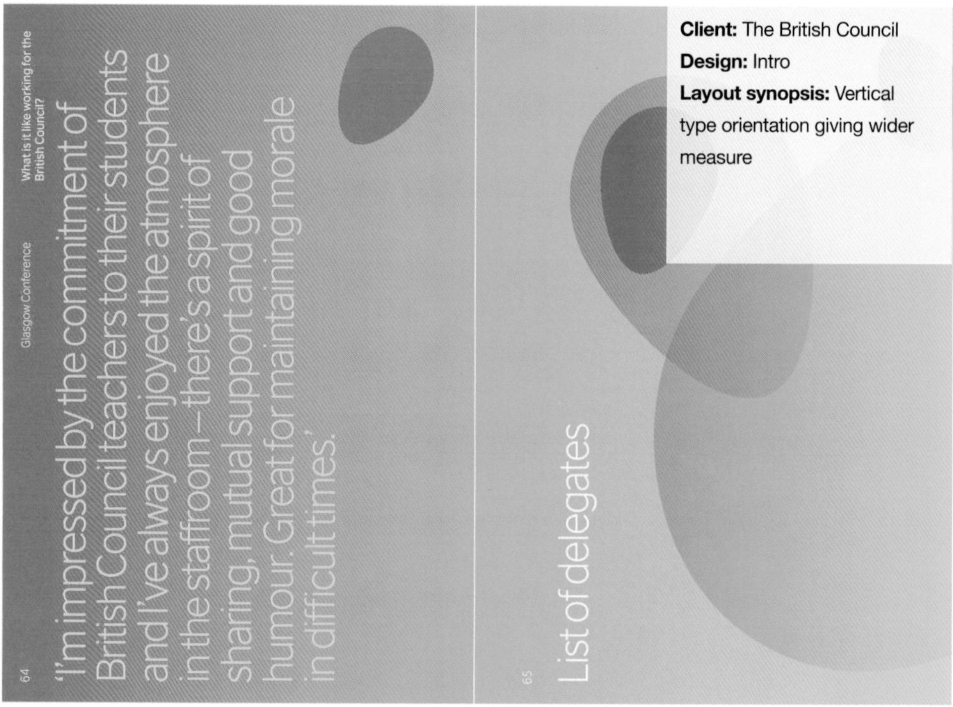

Client: The British Council
Design: Intro
Layout synopsis: Vertical type orientation giving wider measure

Glasgow Conference Brochure

This is a conference brochure produced for The British Council by Intro design studio. The vertical orientation of the type creates a dynamic and lucid series of spreads with a wider measure of the two columns of body text.

The large point size of the font makes this type measure manageable and creates an obvious and distinct hierarchy to the text elements.

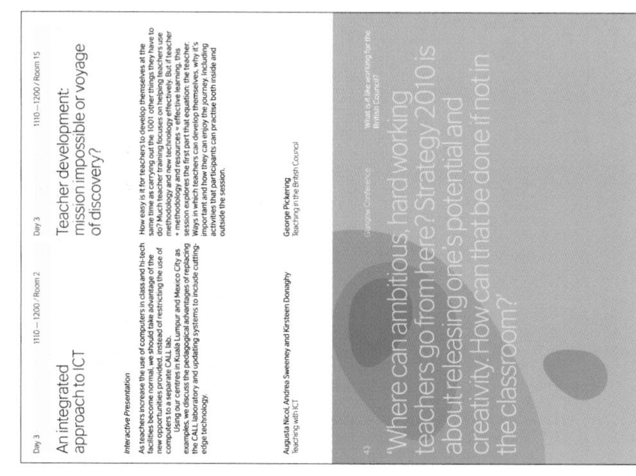

Client: Arnolfini
Design: Thirteen
Layout synopsis: Horizontal body text, vertical captioning

Arnolfini Annual Review

This is the 2002/03 Annual Review for Arnolfini, considered by many as Bristol's premier contemporary art space – designed by Thirteen.

Thirteen created a compact and book-like design for the publication with the jacket doubling as poster artwork. This was a collaboration with artist Andrew Mania and features a picture commemorating the death of poet Thomas Chatterton. The cover was left devoid of text so as not to detract from the artwork but also to invite the reader to open the publication and find out what it contains. Inside, the body copy is presented in horizontal text blocks but captioning for the various illustrations was oriented, but to read vertically as can be seen (left).

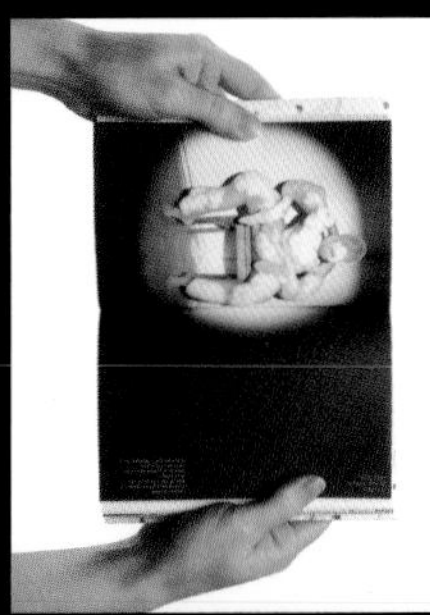

Dividing the page

Dividing a page allows the designer to treat it as a series of connected modules, rather than a single unit, by apportioning space for the various elements the design needs to contain. The partitions can be given individual or collective treatment to deal with related or unrelated material through the use of a grid.

Tate Modern (right)

This brochure, designed for London's Tate Modern by North, features a series of video stills that are used as background images throughout the publication. A series of blocks intersect these images to create a clear space for the placement of text and architectural diagrams.

Client: Tate Modern
Design: North
Layout synopsis: Blocks intersecting background images for text and diagram placement

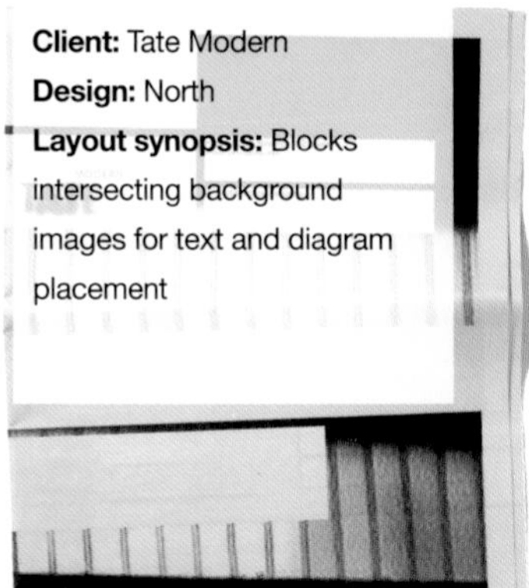

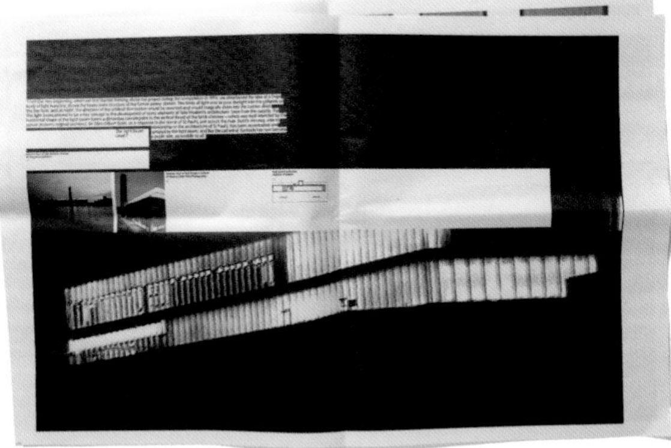

Client: Deutsche Bank
Design: Spin
Layout synopsis:
Typographical placement dictated by constant graphic element

Shipped Ships

Shipped Ships I and *Shipped Ships II* is a two-part publication produced on behalf of the Deutsche Bank by Spin design studio. The books explore the Moment project by artist Ayşe Erkmen. This project saw small ships brought into Frankfurt, Germany from other cities to operate on the Main River for a short period before returning home.

The books have a line running through each page that becomes wider and narrower, changing its dimensions just as a river does. All information is arranged around this key graphic feature that at times provides a space for typographical elements, or otherwise dictates their position.

Client: DWW
Design: Faydherbe / De Vringer
Layout synopsis: Layout incorporating a central timeline theme

DWW Jubilee

Faydherbe / De Vringer was asked to design a publication to celebrate the 75th anniversary of DWW, an organisation linked to the Dutch government and responsible for the road and waterway infrastructure in the Netherlands.

As the client was celebrating an anniversary, Faydherbe / De Vringer created a timeline that passes through the book as a central component of the design. On the cover this line carries the dates of the anniversary: 1927–2002. This band anchors the layout and provides a consistent positioning reference throughout the work.

Timeline
A timeline is a graphic representation of the history of something such as a person or organisation. It denotes key events in that history in a sequential order. In these spreads (below), the timeline is a visual device and unifying element of the designs.

Client: CCAC
Design: Aufuldish + Warinner
Layout synopsis: Different-sized blocks for text and images. Varied treatments for captions, footnotes, folios and running heads

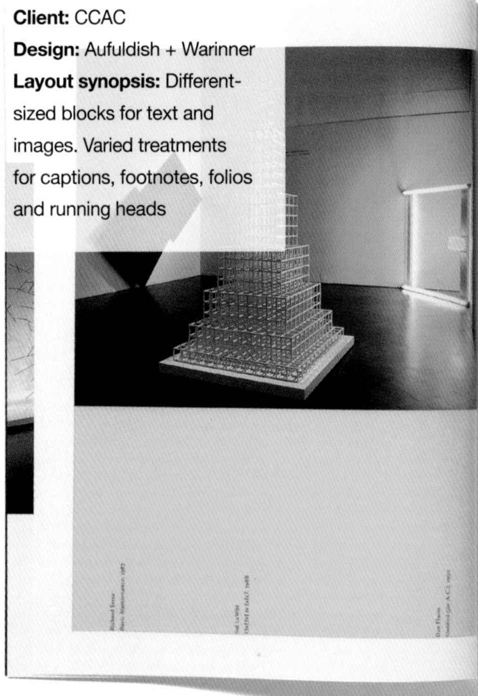

RETROSPECTACLE Selected Object Entries

MIROSLAW BALKA

Polish, born 1958, Warsaw;
lives in Otwock, Poland

190 x 60 x 4, 190 x 60 x 4, 190 x 50 x 40, 190 x 50 x 40, 190 x 50 x 40, 50 x 40 x 1, 1992

Steel, brass, salt, ash, foam, carpet, and felt;
overall dimensions variable;
three elements on wall at 75 ¼ x 20 x 16 inches;
two on floor at 1 ¼ x 75 x 23 ¼ inches

Funds from 1994 Alliance for Contemporary Art Auction, 1994.462

Though the "arte povera" attitude to materials informs his work, Balka's approach is more personal than ideological, being deeply rooted in the poverty of his Cold War, Eastern European youth. Balka's sculptures have a quiet, compelling presence. They are human scaled–the title of this work not only denotes actual dimensions of each of its five parts but refers to the artist's own body measurements; in fact all of the pieces appear as strange bodily containers, if not in fact coffins. As an artist who lived much of his life in a house that seems impossibly tiny by our standards, Balka is obsessed with the body's relationship to the spaces it inhabits and the objects it uses. This sculpture's thin, distressed sheets of steel–anointed with small pads of felt, scraps of paper, and minuscule amounts of salt–evoke domestic impoverishment. It also indicates poignant allusions to the body: small, awkwardly placed holes in the two horizontal elements mark eyes, navel, and toes, as if these slabs were death beds or coffin lids, and these specks are all that's left of decomposed bodies. The holes are filled with salt–a life sustaining substance, but also the residue of evaporated bodily fluids like sweat or tears.

The vertical elements have holes as well but with other implications, a shower drain or peep holes, references, perhaps, to holocaust gas chambers. That the elements are either upright or prone accentuates the blunt fact of two possibilities: being alive and being dead, or alternatively, suffering in life and past suffering of those now dead. The plain, rectangular forms are not truly minimalist because they are sort of proxy human beings. —MJ

JOHN DEANDREA

American, born 1941, Denver;
lives in Denver

Clothed Artist and Model, 1976

Polychromed vinyl, clothing, plaster, and hair,
75 x 96 x 96 inches

Gift of William and Vivian Jaeger, 1989.273

The Denver Art Museum's other major DeAndrea sculpture, *Linda*, from 1984, is one of the most asked-for works in the collection. *Linda* could be DeAndrea's Galatea: a lifelike, idealized, sleeping nude woman. She only needs a kiss to wake up. Though just as magically realistic, *Clothed Artist and Model* further poses questions about such realism. It incorporates an ironic comment about the artistic working process and reveals a great deal about the artist himself. The illusion gets doubled because the sculpture depicts a moment in its own making. The finished sculpture of the model sits fully nude and encased in the bottom half of her own plaster mold, while the finished sculpture of the artist, having just slathered this mold on the model, contemplates his work in progress with residual plaster nearly encasing his own hands. But of course the reflective nature of the work is staged, and it is hard to deny the sexual intimation in the artist's gaze and the model's posture. An idealization in progress, perhaps, but the tableau depicts the reality behind the realism. The model might be fully exposing her body to the artist and to the viewer, but DeAndrea's self-portrait–what this piece really is–is unforgiving. —MJ

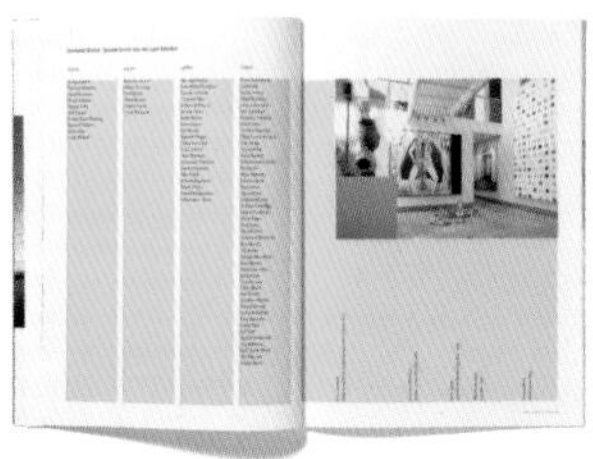

Insights / Dialogues

This brochure for the Colorado Contemporary Arts Collaboration, designed by Aufuldish + Warinner, uses different-sized yellow blocks to delineate the space for text and images. All body text is justified, whilst captions and footnotes are range right. The footnotes create small squares at the base of the columns (bottom row, left). Folio numbers are centred and the running head appears on the far right of the recto page. Text in some blocks runs vertically.

Client: Semoma
Design: Aufuldish + Warinner
Layout synopsis: Rigid grid with experimental flourishes, various treatments for captions, headers and folio numbers

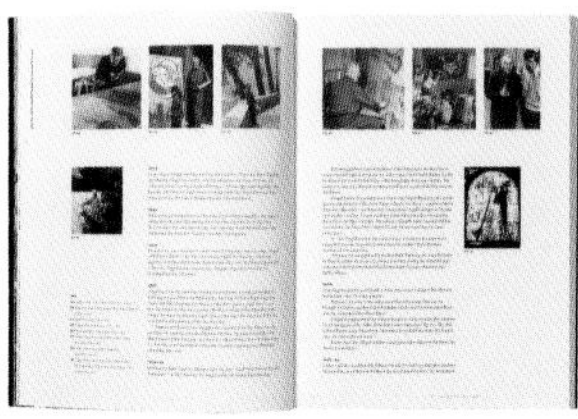

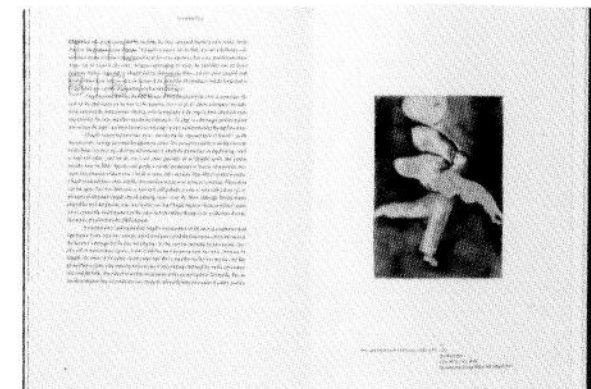

Marc Chagall

This is a book designed by Aufuldish + Warinner for Semoma about Russian-born French artist Marc Chagall. The book contains archival photography and plates. The large full-colour plates sit in white space whilst the photography forms part of a more complex layout. The images sit at the top of the page in boxes, with the occasional photograph bleeding off the page. The grid is rigid but has experimental touches. Folio numbers are centred with an adjacent running head that appears on the recto page only. Underneath the colour plates, captions range right whilst additional information ranges left.

Client: Diesel
Design: KesselsKramer
Layout synopsis: Full-page statements

Diesel

The cover of this publication, created by KesselsKramer design studio on behalf of clothing manufacturer Diesel, is treated as one integral canvas (rather than as adjacent recto and verso pages), across which a message is plastered in handwritten letters. Little consideration is afforded to positioning or avoidance of the central gutter. However, the slogans are central and vertically aligned to further enhance visibility.

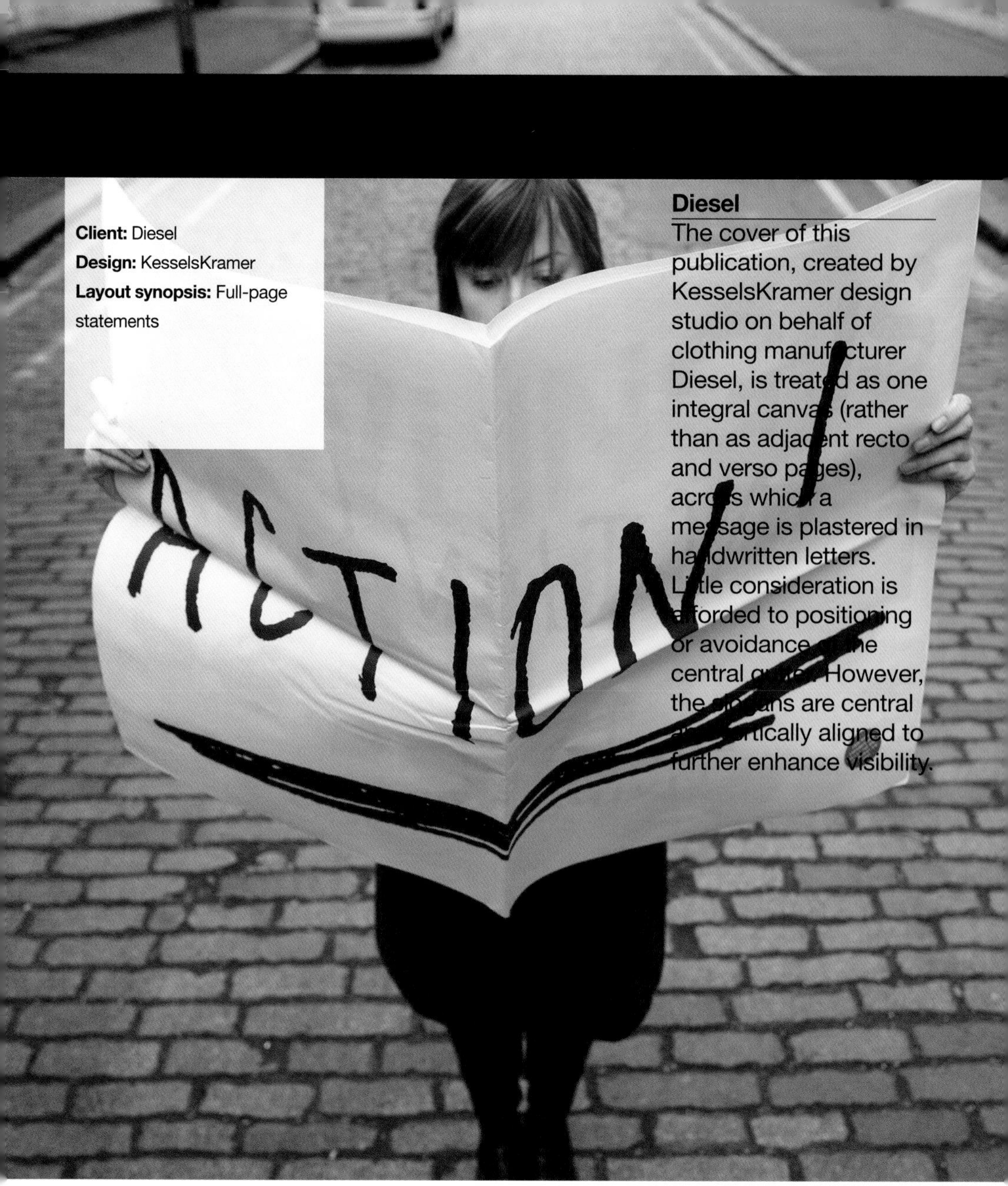

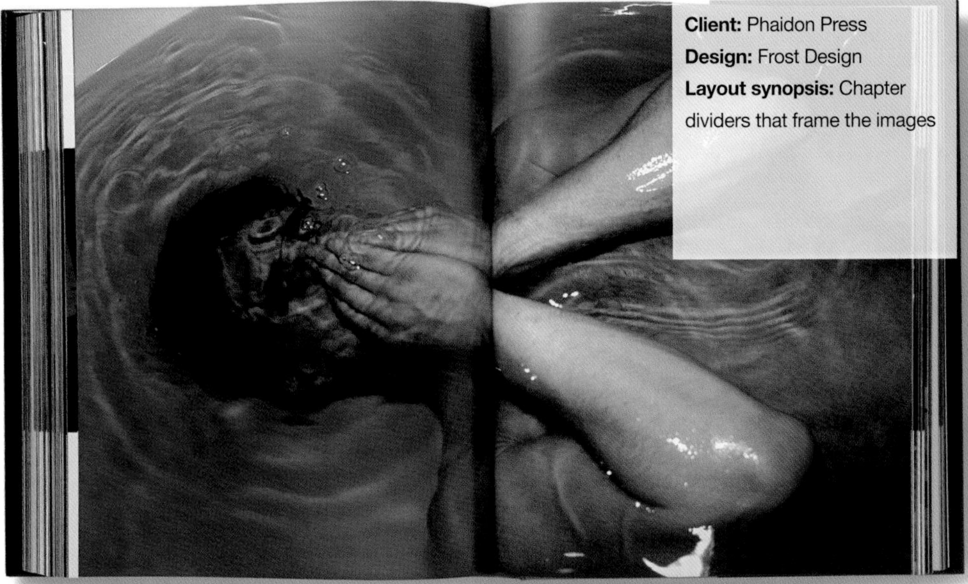

The Devil's Playground

Nan Goldin's photographic book features themed chapters of personal and intimate images. The chapters are separated by texts, poems and lyrics by writers such as Nick Cave and Catherine Lampert. Frost Design created chapter title pages using plain colours, which are sympathetic to the rich colours of the images and that help frame them.

Structure / unstructure

Layout concerns the structuring of elements on a page so that they can communicate effectively with a reader. Absence of a structure can also be used to good effect to convey certain characteristics in a design – although this in itself is also a type of structure.

Unstructured designs can be some of the most visually creative and, by definition, are more difficult to control in order to achieve the desired results.

When deconstructing fundamental layout principles to create an unstructured work a designer must consider whether the intended target audience will be able to identify and access the information it contains.

Client: NEROC'VGM
Design: KesselsKramer
Layout synopsis: Simple structure using passe partout

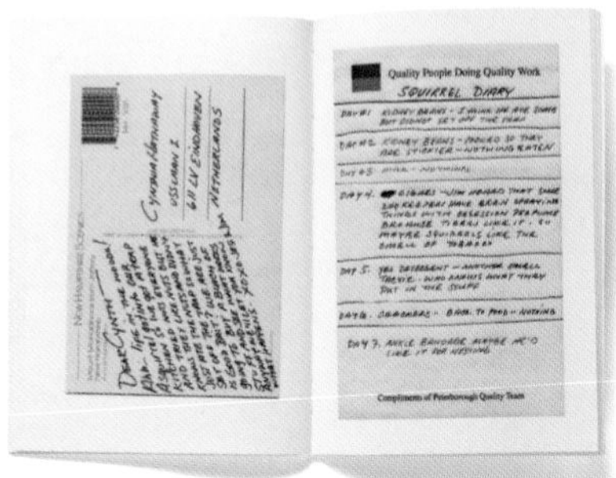

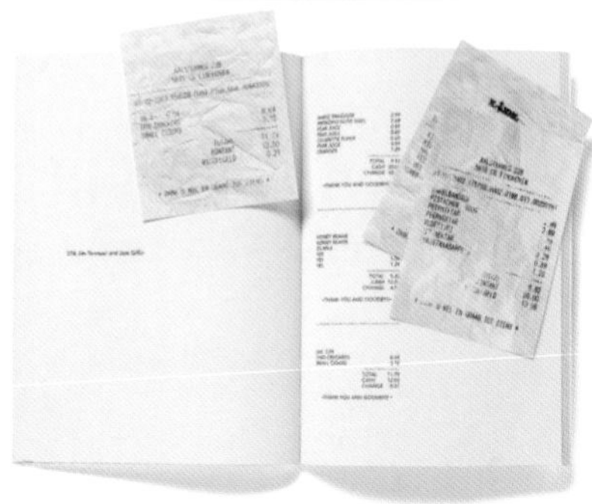

A Meeting in the Supermarket

A Meeting in the Supermarket by Cynthia Hathaway is a book produced for the Dutch marketing communications company NEROC'VGM, which contains short narratives, or 'sliptales', created by 13 designers and themed around a supermarket. Elements such as parking spaces, receipts, tills, shelves and so on are the starting point for these imaginative interpretations.

KesselsKramer used a fairly simple structure to order and present these different, and sometimes unstructured, pieces in book form. Passe partout framing and minimum design intervention allow the works to speak for themselves.

Client: Hawkins \ Brown
Design: SEA Design
Layout synopsis: Basic structure to splice together elements

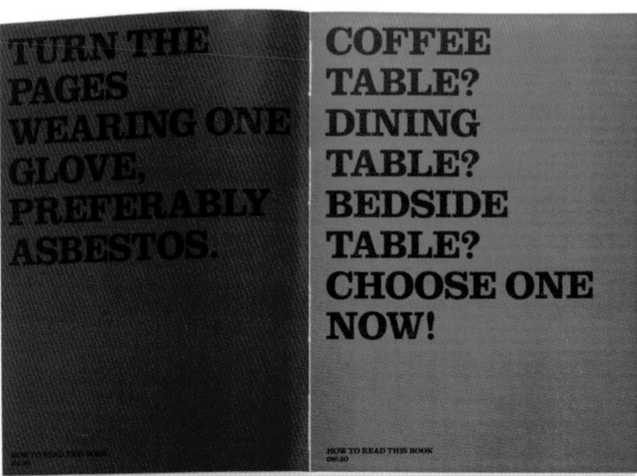

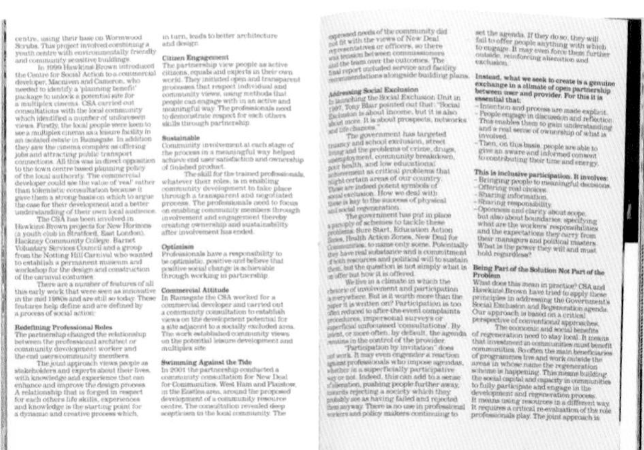

& \ also

This book, created by SEA Design on behalf of London architects Hawkins \ Brown explores the creativity, diversity and tenacity of contemporary architecture.

The publication uses a basic structure to splice together images, which detail everyday objects, pose questions and give instructions that induce the reader to think.

Cirkus Humberto (right)

This book, designed by Browns and featuring photographs by Bettina von Kameke, documents the people involved in Cirkus Humberto. The circus supplied posters for the publication that were then folded and used for the cover, which is vibrant, thoughtful and unique. As the poster folds through the centre of the clown's face, the front cover presents a wink whilst the back cover carries a laughing eye. A simple passe partout contains the images and captions running vertically in a sans serif font.

Client: Bettina von Kameke
Design: Browns
Layout synopsis: Poster cover positioning, passe partout photograph presentation, vertical captions

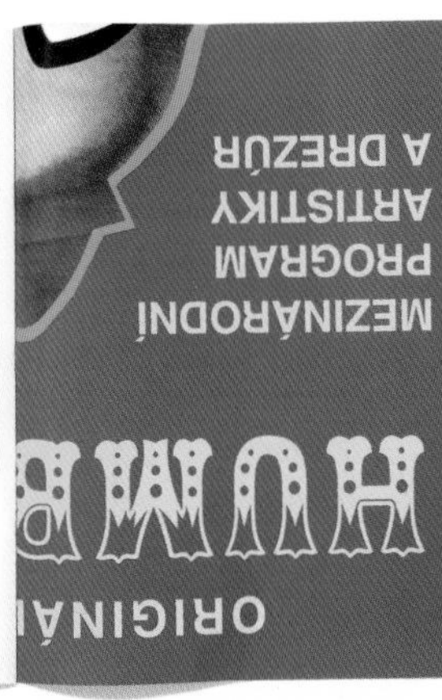

Paper engineering

Paper engineering addresses some of the format decisions designers make in order to produce the end result. The format of a publication can open new possibilities for an innovative use of layout; as these examples show.

Format elements such as binding and folding options pose additional layout issues that the designer must resolve.

Lanagraphic (right)

This brochure for Zanders Papers by Roundel design studio features photography by Richard Learoyd. The textures, finishes and weights of papers produced by Zanders are explained visually in the publication, which has cut-short and interleaved sections. A visual analogy is used to describe a product that might have been difficult to make interesting, as on successive pages an apple passes from being whole to being half-eaten. The outside paper stock is a textured felt that associates with the skin of the apple, whilst the inside stock is smooth and so relates to the soft flesh of the apple.

Client: Zanders Papers
Design: Roundel
Layout synopsis: Repeated image placement combined with different paper stocks for visual analogy

OUTSIDE

Smooth
Soft White 240gsm
CMYK

INSIDE

Smooth
Cascade White 135gsm
CMYK

OUTSIDE

Smooth
Soft White 240gsm
CMYK

Client: NEROC'VGM
Design: KesselsKramer
Layout synopsis: Gatefold featuring passe partout image, four-module grid

A Meeting on the Street

This is a book designed by KesselsKramer for NEROC'VGM, a Dutch marketing communications company. It features a series of photographs taken by Hans Eijeklboom of mothers and daughters out shopping on consecutive Saturday afternoons in the cities of Amsterdam, Paris, Berlin and London.

Each spread has a gatefold section featuring a large, single passe partout image. The entire book is set on a four-module grid enforcing the idea that it is a collection, or album, of images.

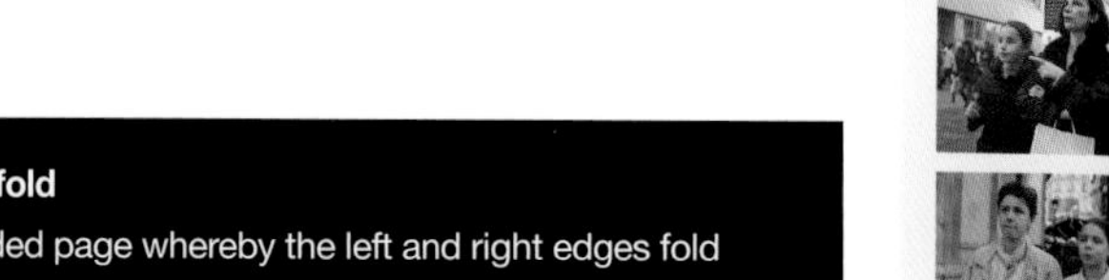

Gatefold
A folded page whereby the left and right edges fold inward with parallel folds and meet in the middle of the page without overlapping.

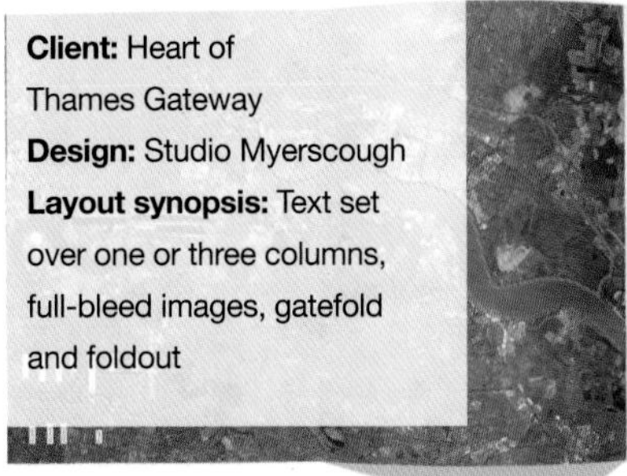

Client: Heart of Thames Gateway
Design: Studio Myerscough
Layout synopsis: Text set over one or three columns, full-bleed images, gatefold and foldout

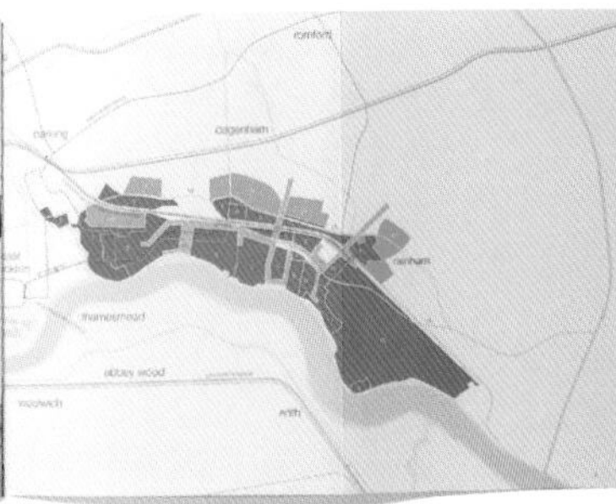

An Urban Strategy for London Riverside

This brochure designed by Studio Myerscough outlines a strategy for a development on the banks of London's River Thames. An aerial photograph printed on a two-panel gatefold at the front complements a three-panel foldout at the back, which contains an illustration of the proposed development.

The body has a simple layout, with introductory sections set in a single column at the top of the page. A three-column grid contains secondary supporting information. Images appear full-bleed, or as two half-page full-bleeds (bottom right).

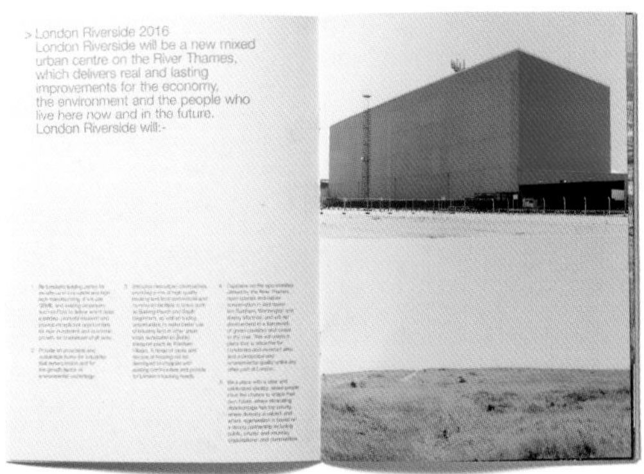

Client: Building Sights
Design: Studio Myerscough
Layout synopsis: Z-bind to form physical separation

Z-bind

A z-bind is used to join two book blocks together with a single cover. It is named after the shape of the folded cover, which forms a 'z' with one book block nesting in each internal angle. Book blocks may then be bound in with a variety of binding methods including saddle-stitch, elastic and perfect.

Client: Harper Mackay
Design: Form Design
Layout synopsis: Accordion fold dictating image placement, vertical text orientation

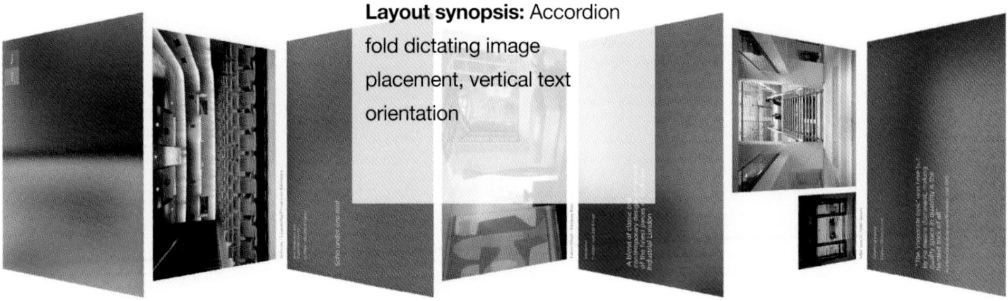

Harper Mackay (above)

This mailer for architectural practice Harper Mackay by Form Design has an accordion fold. It features a series of atmospheric images of interiors that are positioned on alternate panels of the fold. These are separated by colour panels containing brief textural information, which is set vertically.

Building the Jubilee School (left)

This book, created by Studio Myerscough for Building Sights, is a record of the construction of a school in Brixton, London by Allford Hall Monaghan Morris. A type of z-bind was used to join the two parts and form a separation between them, although the extra cover panels actually form a 'w'. The first part of the book discusses the construction process, whilst the second part deals with the design process. The central joining panel is a schedule of key events in the entire process culminating with the opening ceremony.

Building Sights is a project funded by the English Arts Council and the Commission for Architecture and the Built Environment (CABE).

Client: E A Shaw
Design: Imagination
Layout synopsis: Different-sized outer for theme separation

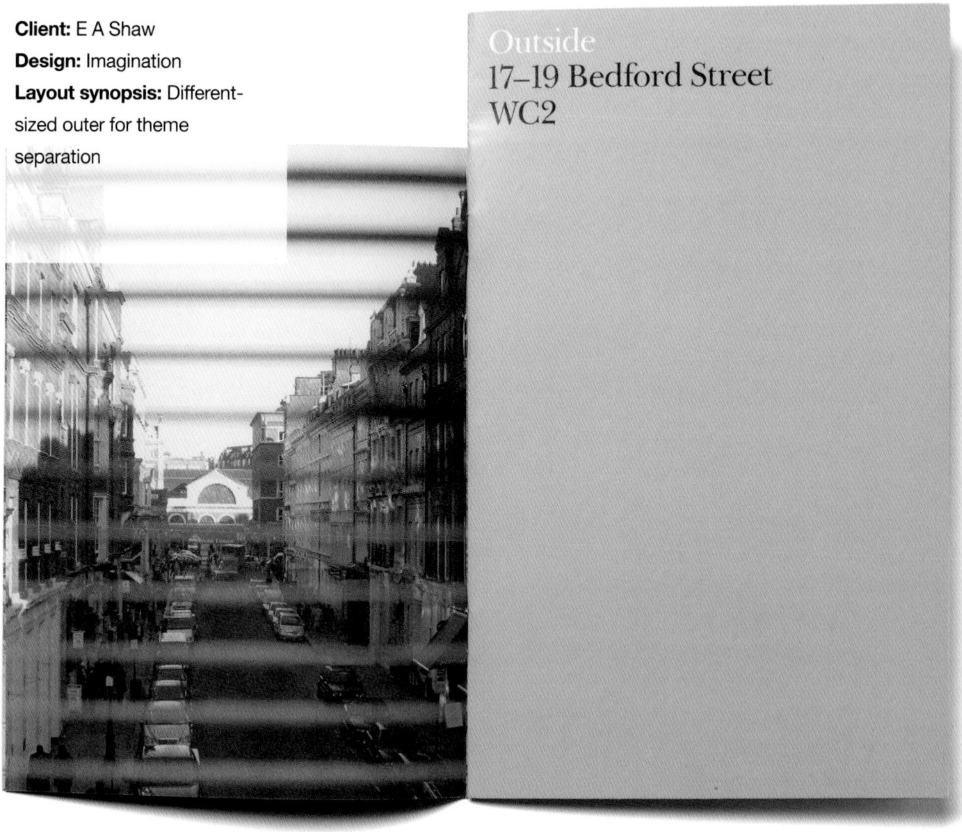

Outside
17–19 Bedford Street
WC2

17–19 Bedford Street

This is a brochure designed by Imagination on behalf of E A Shaw to promote the 17–19 Bedford Street WC2 property development in London. The brochure has interleaved pages, which are cut short and flush at the bottom of the document. The cover of the publication focuses on the area surrounding the development, whilst inner pages focus on the building itself. The ultimate aim is to sell the location as much as the building.

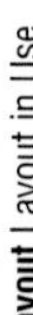

Inside Outside

This is a promotional brochure for the Lanagraphic product of Zanders Papers and was created by Roundel design studio. The interior features themed images that are viewed from the inside, such as a pair of slippers, a baby in the womb and a Scalextric racing game. Conversely, the exterior features images themed on things that are found 'outside', such as a dustbin, blades of grass and a park bench. The publication is bound dos-à-dos (back to back).

The spread below (left) features two images from the inside part of the publication; the spread on the right features two images from the outside part of the publication.

Client: Zanders Papers
Design: Roundel
Layout synopsis: Binding to create physical separation

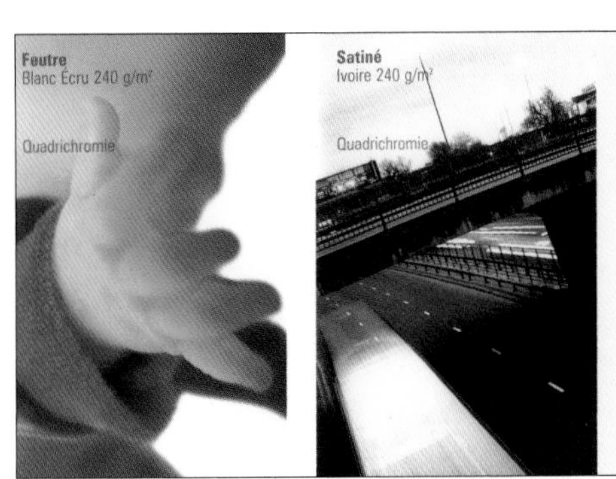

Passe partout

Passe partout historically refers to the cardboard mount that sits between a picture and the glass when one frames an image. The term can also be applied to the borders or the white space around the outside edge of a page or design element.

A border helps to define the space on a page and the relationships between the items it contains, and into which a design can comfortably be placed. This section explores some of the ways passe partout can be used to help structure page layout.

Client: Phaidon Press
Design: Gavin Ambrose
Layout synopsis: Full-cropped images within simple, standard frame

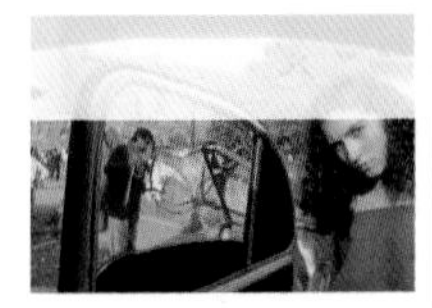

A Way into India

The spreads above are taken from the book *A Way into India* by Raghubir Singh and designed by Gavin Ambrose for Phaidon Press. All images are shown full crop and the layout was closely based on the pagination established by Raghubir Singh as he collected and collated the images in a scrapbook. A consistent passe partout is applied throughout the book as part of the deliberate, minimal design input used to create a simple, pure layout that allows the pictures to speak for themselves.

Every image features an Ambassador, a car that is common to India. The car either forms part of the subject matter or is the medium through which the subject matter has been photographed. At a different level the abstract parts of the car, the window frame through which something has been photographed, also act as a border. White pages provide a visual pause as there are no chapters or breaker pages.

Client: Evisu
Design: George & Vera
Layout synopsis: Simple white border on every page

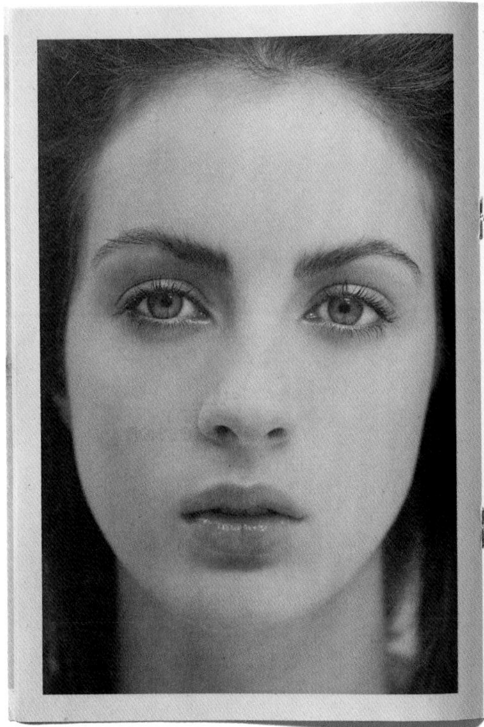

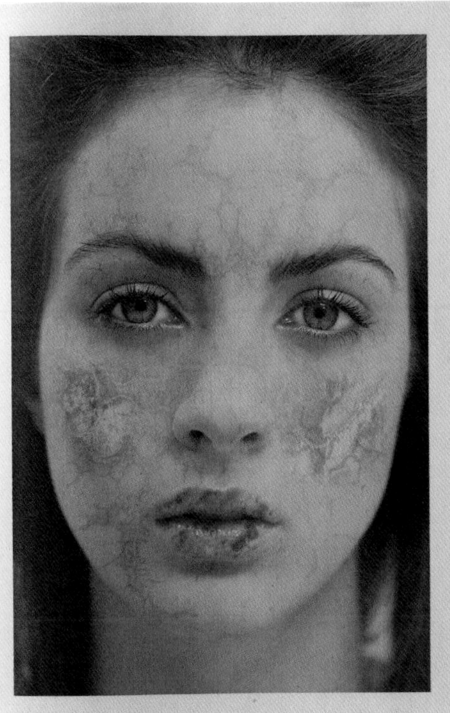

Intellectual property

This is a catalogue for an intellectual property exhibition featuring images by artist Larry Dunstan and designed by George & Vera for Evisu. A simple passe partout is used on every page to provide a consistent and equal setting for each image. The series of single colour prints becomes framed by the space surrounding it. This direct framing establishes a juxtaposition of images in a sterile and unemotional manner.

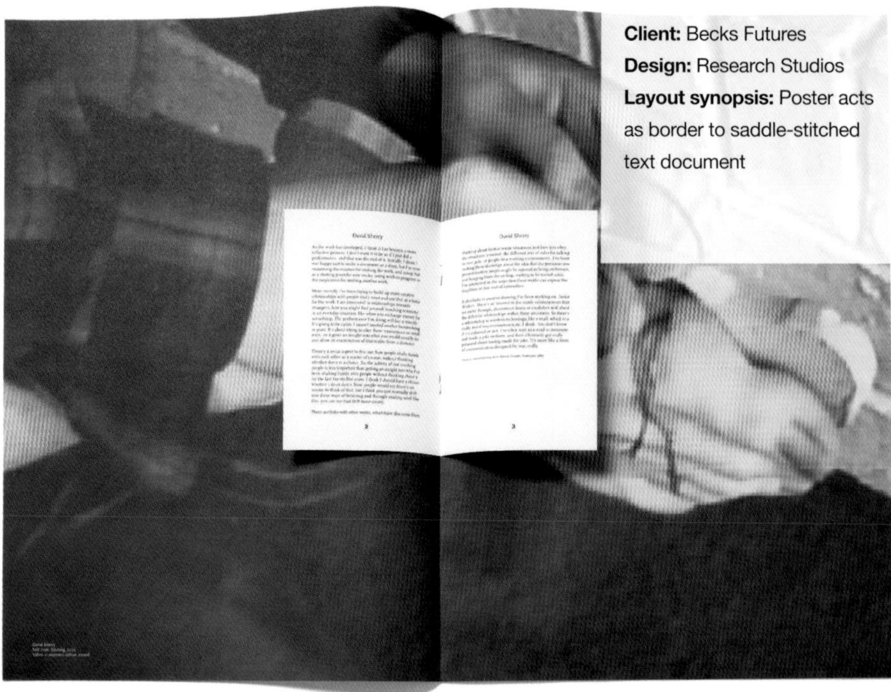

Client: Becks Futures
Design: Research Studios
Layout synopsis: Poster acts as border to saddle-stitched text document

Client: Corbis
Design: Segura Inc.
Layout synopsis: Juxtaposed archival images inset in a passe partout

Future (above)

The Corbis *Future* brochure by Segura Inc. features a series of images that depicts the company's interpretation of the future. Displayed within passe partout borders these pictures present a surreal and abstract series of narratives.

Becks Futures (left)

This brochure for Becks Futures features printed text documents saddle stitched into the fold of a poster. Each poster is a large-scale screengrab of one of the entries to the contest. As such, the art forms a fantastically disproportionate border for the text pieces that it frames.

Juxtaposition

Juxtaposition is the deliberate placement of contrasting images side by side. The word is formed from the Latin 'juxta', which means near, and 'position'.

In graphic design and page layout juxtaposition may be used to present two or more ideas so as to impart a relationship between them, as seen in the example opposite. Here, the relationship concerns the shape of the two objects and the sensation their position suggests.

Juxtaposition may imply similarity or dissimilarity, demonstrating that two things are essentially the same or quite different. This may only be clear from the context of the work as a whole. Many designers use juxtaposition in their work with the implicit intention that readers work out the connection themselves.

Sensation (right)

This poster for the *Sensation* exhibition at the Royal Academy of Arts in London was designed by Why Not Associates and is a simple juxtaposition of two images that ordinarily do not belong together. The tongue and iron have similar shapes, but there is more at work here. The tongue appears to be touching the iron; this would cause a painfully hot sensation if the iron were switched on and so we may recoil in discomfort at the idea the image suggests by association. *Sensation* featured many controversial, contemporary art works and therefore the poster suggests the extreme nature of some of the exhibits.

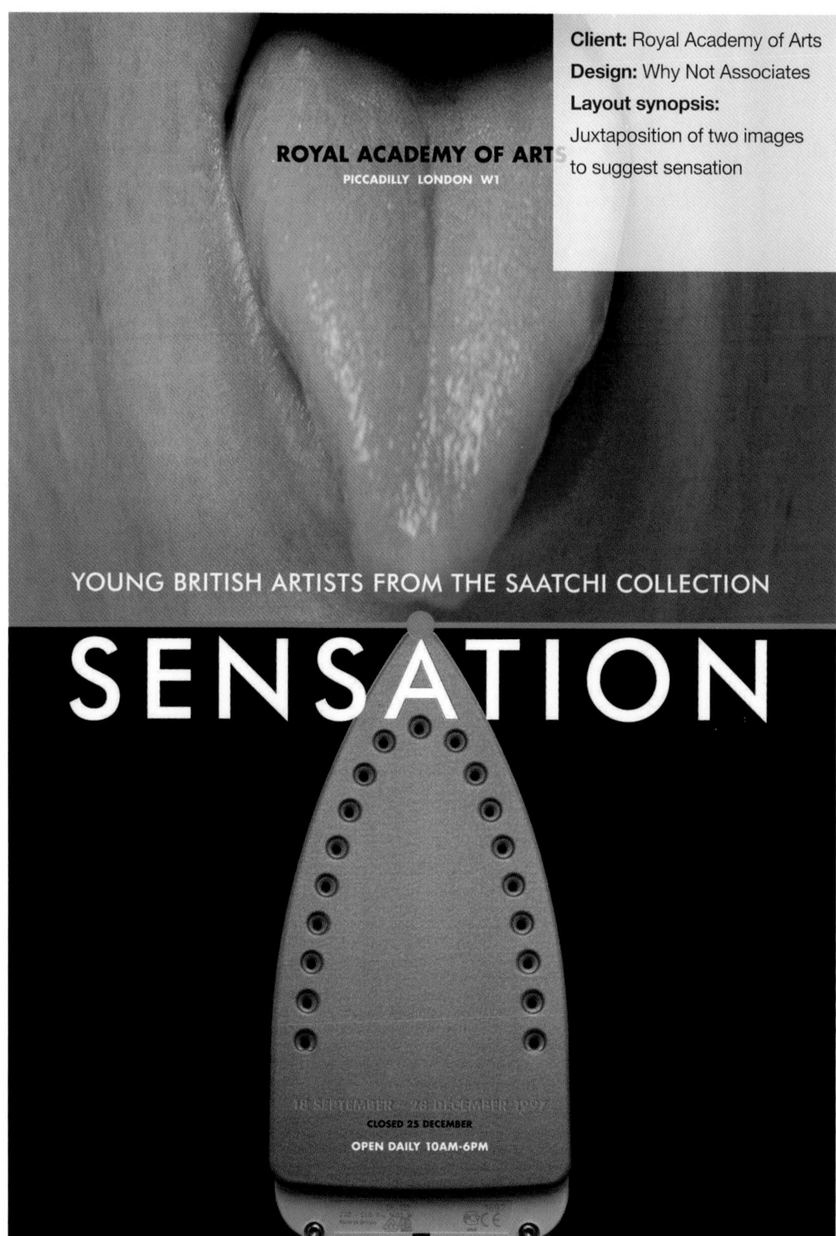

Client: Royal Academy of Arts
Design: Why Not Associates
Layout synopsis: Juxtaposition of two images to suggest sensation

Impart

Ideas can be expressed implicitly or they can be suggested (or imparted) through the presentation of information that the reader decodes in order to arrive at the required interpretation. In the example above, a juxtaposition of two images is used to impart the idea of sensation.

Zanders Papers

This is a brochure for Zanders Papers designed by Roundel and features photography by Trevor Ray Hart. The brochure juxtaposes images of the four elements – earth, water, fire and air – with four paper finishes – fibre linen, hammer and wove.

The resulting collision of seemingly unrelated images is both surreal and engaging. The simple use of arresting typography further adds to the debasing of understanding. Only upon closer inspection do we realise that 'HAMMER' relates to the paper finish, and not the image.

Client: Zanders Papers
Design: Roundel
Layout synopsis:
Juxtaposition of images and paper finishes

Client: Ben®

Design: KesselsKramer

Layout synopsis:

Juxtaposition of portraits and surroundings

Ben® (left)

This is a book of 'Bens' produced for the Dutch Mobile phone company Ben®, and designed by KesselsKramer.

All the 'Bens' featured are from Salt Lake City, USA. Portrait photographs are juxtaposed on a double-page spread against an image of their surroundings. This provides a very disjointed and surreal, yet interesting impression.

Maidstone Alternative Urban Living (right)

This promotional brochure for the town of Maidstone, England was created by Studio Myerscough to showcase the benefits of buying property in the town. It is printed as a series of folded loose-leaf posters that provide some interesting image collisions. Thus we see a woman reading juxtaposed with a glamorous shoe, implying socialising, and people eating alfresco against historical elements implying the combination of tradition and modern values.

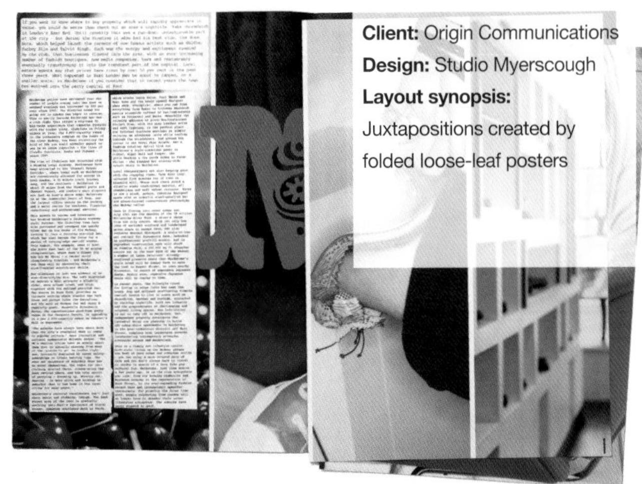

Client: Origin Communications

Design: Studio Myerscough

Layout synopsis:

Juxtapositions created by folded loose-leaf posters

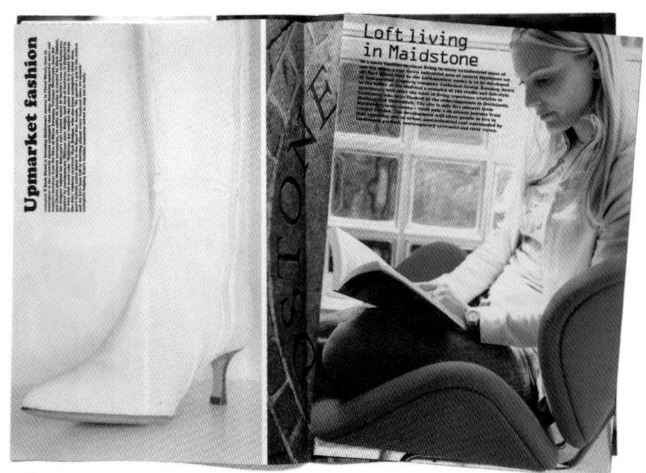

Client: Derwent Valley
Design: Studio Myerscough
Layout synopsis: Spacious layout to reflect content, random text placement

Tea Building
Shoreditch E1

Breaking the Rules

This volume outlines some of the fundamental layout principles that graphic designers use to produce effective designs for a variety of different purposes and clients.

Using the basics allows a designer to make informed decisions and use time efficiently and effectively. Graphic design is a creative activity and there are therefore occasions when breaking the rules is necessary in order to meet the design brief.

The following pages showcase how some contemporary designers break the rules.

'Every part of a text relates to every other part by a definite, logical relationship of emphasis and value, predetermined by content. It is up to the typographer to express this relationship clearly and visibly, through type sizes and weight, arrangement of lines, use of colour, photography etc.'
Jan Tschichold

The Tea Building (left)

Property brochures are normally quite conservative, but for this piece for Derwent Valley that promotes The Tea Building in London, Studio Myerscough used a mixture of typeset and hand-scrawled typography to overlay a series of atmospheric photographs by Richard Learoyd. Space in the building was rented as empty shells, which the designer made a focal aspect of the design. These empty spaces translate into open and empty spreads and the lack of finishing details in the building translates into rough, handwritten typography. Text blocks are randomly placed wherever there is free space.

Working without a grid

A grid provides a structure and constraints within which a design is to be arranged. At times the use of a grid is not appropriate, perhaps due to the nature of the material to be presented, or the visual effect that the designer wants to produce.

Abandoning the grid allows greater freedom and creativity to be unleashed, although the designer still needs to control this in order to avoid a somewhat dysfunctional result.

If working without a grid the designer may still be guided by an underlying principle or theme of the work to assist the decision-making process. In this way structure is still provided but it is not dictated by a grid.

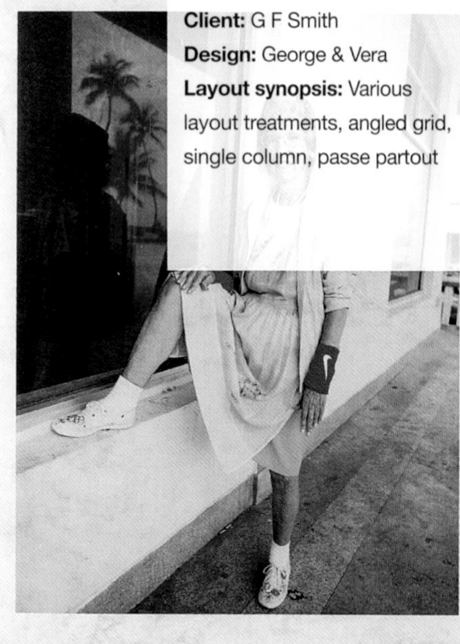

Client: G F Smith
Design: George & Vera
Layout synopsis: Various layout treatments, angled grid, single column, passe partout

Rude KruelSummer Spring/Summer 2004

KruelSummer is a collaboration between George & Vera, paper producer G F Smith and Rude. It features works by known and emerging artists, photographers and designers and showcases a series of innovative paper stocks produced by G F Smith.

The publication presents a diverse set of layouts, type styles and other design elements to produce an eclectic result. This includes angled layouts through to single type columns running into the gutter.

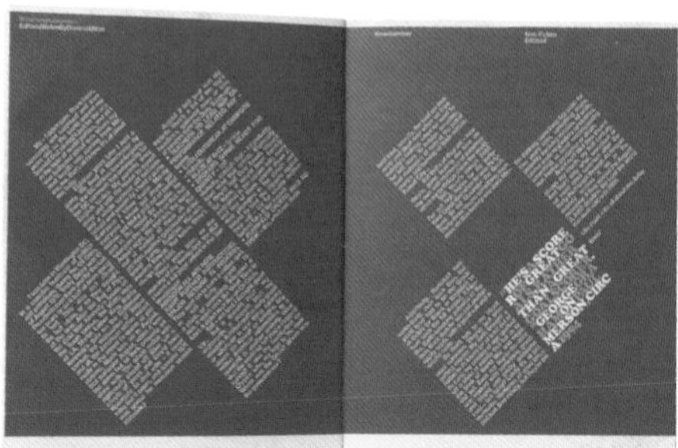

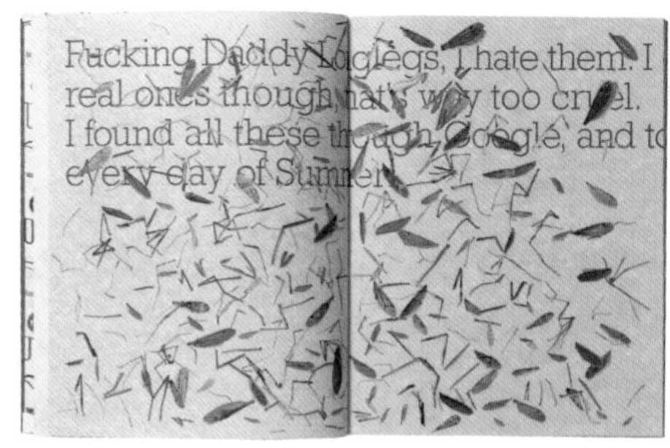

Client: DTI, Trade Partners UK, British Council
Design: Studio Myerscough
Layout synopsis: Free-flowing text, overprints

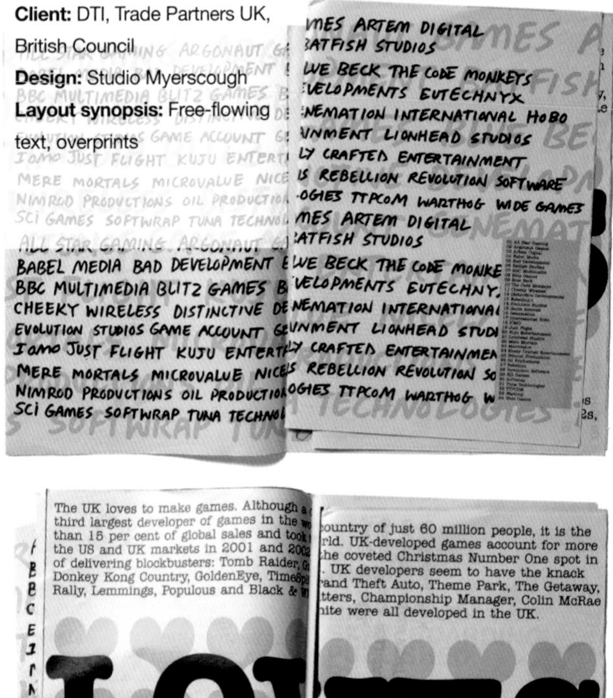

UK: State of Play (left)

The UK: State of Play pavilion at the E3 interactive entertainment trade event promotes the UK's best computer-games companies. This pavilion brochure designed by Studio Myerscough uses text and images that flow across double-page spreads and black type overprinted on a yellow background to obtain an unstructured, youthful and dynamic feel to correspond with the energy of the gaming industry.

Zembla Magazine (right)

Zembla is an international literary magazine. The layout for this issue was intentionally created without a grid by Frost Design. The absence of a grid offers great diversity in the flow and pace of the publication and allows the designers to use specific graphic approaches for individual spreads. This is particularly practical given that the content is so varied and changeable.

Client: Zembla

Design: Frost Design

Layout synopsis: Gridless to provide diversity, pace variation, handle varied content

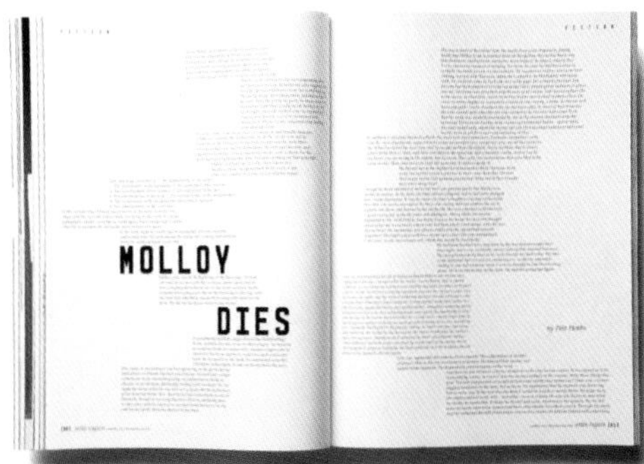

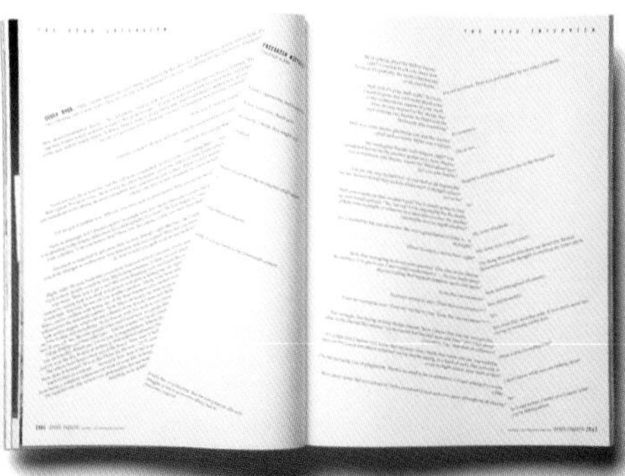

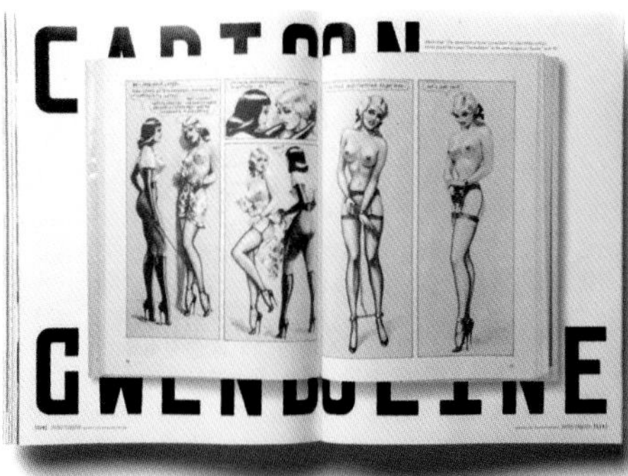

Glossary

The subject of layout contains many technical terms that can be confusing and overwhelming. This glossary is intended to define some of the most common technical terms in usage in order to facilitate a better understanding and appreciation of the subject, although it will be far from exhaustive.

An understanding of the terms used in layout can help in the articulation of creative ideas to other designers, to commissioning clients, as well as printers and other professionals that will work to produce the design. The knowledge and use of standard industry terms minimises the risk of any misunderstanding that could complicate or even ruin a job.

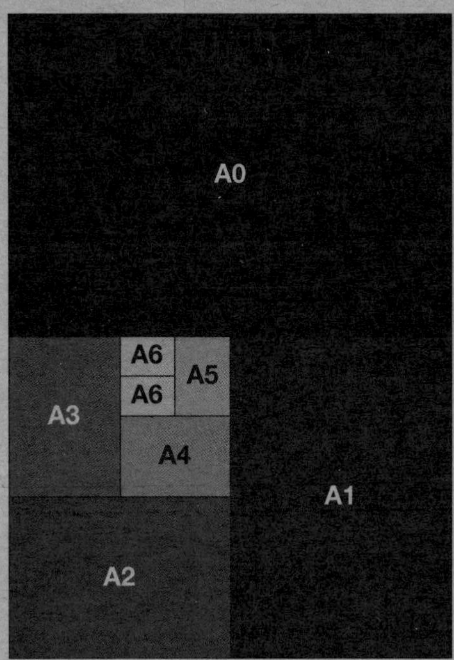

A-series paper sizes

4A0	1680mm x 2376mm
2A0	1189mm x 1681mm
A0	841mm x 1189mm
A1	594mm x 841mm
A2	420mm x 594mm
A3	297mm x 420mm
A4	210mm x 297mm
A5	148mm x 210mm
A6	105mm x 148mm
A7	74mm x 105mm
A8	52.5mm x 74mm
A9	37mm x 52.5mm
A10	26.25mm x 37mm

Deutsche Industrie Norm

German Dr Walter Porstmann invented the A, B and C series paper formats that were adopted as the German standard in 1922. This DIN (Deutsche Industrie Norm) standard subsequently became an ISO (International Organization for Standardization) standard and the official United Nations document format in 1975.

A-series paper sizes
ISO metric standard paper size based on the square root of two ratio. The A0 sheet (841mm x 1189mm) is one square metre and each size (A1, A2, A3, A4 etc.) thereafter differs from the next by a factor of either 2 or 1/2.

Accordion or concertina fold
Two or more parallel folds that go in opposite directions and open out like an accordion.

Alignment
Text location within a text block in the vertical and horizontal planes.

Appropriation
The borrowing of a style, typically used elsewhere, as the basis for a design.

Assemblage
An artistic composition made from various odds and ends centred around a given theme or bringing together several different themes.

Asymmetrical grids
A grid that is the same on recto and verso pages and typically introduces a bias towards one side of the page (usually the left).

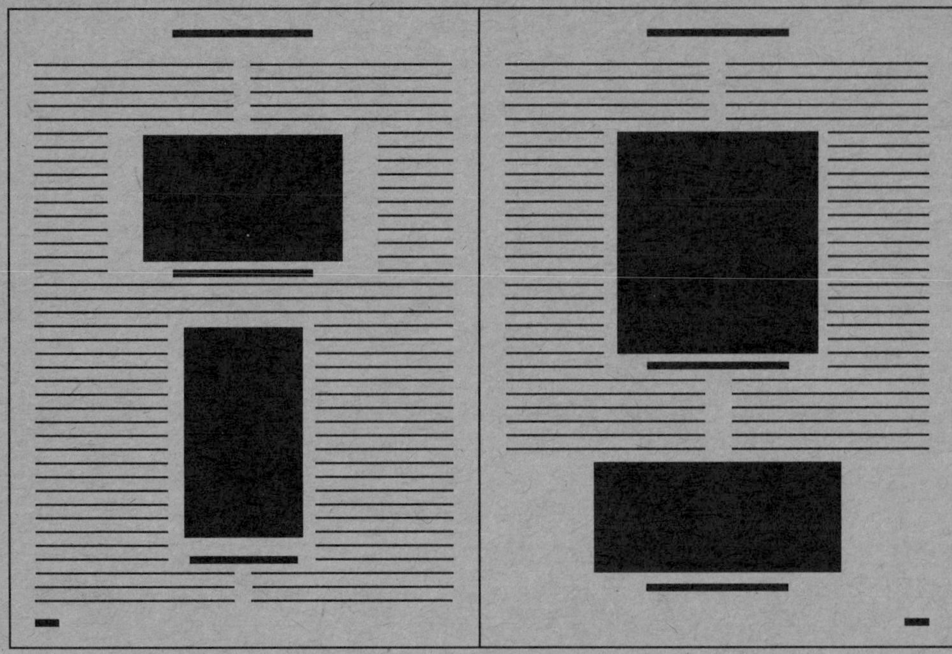

Schematic, thoughtless centring of blocks. Decorative, impractical, uneconomic (= ugly)

The diagrams on this and the facing page are from pioneering Dutch typographer and designer Jan Tschichold's *The New Typography*. Tschichold believes that placing images in such a way that they interfere with a text block wastes space and reduces the overall aesthetic.

B-series paper sizes
ISO metric standard paper size based on the square root of two ratio. B sizes are intermediate sizes to the A-series sizes.

Baseline
The imaginary line upon which the bases of all capital letters and most lower case letters are positioned.

Baseline grid
The graphic foundation on which a design is constructed.

Binding
Any of several processes for holding together the pages or sections of a publication to form a book, magazine, brochure or some other format using stitches, wire, glue or other media.

Bleed
Printed content that extends past where the pages will be trimmed.

Body copy
The matter that forms the predominant textual element of a piece of work.

Captions
Text that describes or names graphic elements.

Constructive, meaningful and economical (= beautiful)

In contrast, when images are placed in consideration of layout guidelines the overall balance is more dynamic and pleasing.

Colour fall
The pages of the publication, as depicted in the imposition plan, which will receive a special colour or varnish or are to be printed on a different stock.

Column
An area or field into which text is flowed.

Cross-alignment
A typographical hierarchy where the different levels share a common relationship and can be aligned in the same grid.

Display type
Large and/or distinctive type that is intended to attract the eye. Specifically cut to be viewed from a distance.

Dummy
Provisional layout showing illustration and text positions as they will appear in the final reproduction.

Exquisite corpse
Surrealist technique that exploits the happy chance of accident in image/text juxtaposition.

Extent
The number of pages in a book.

Fibonacci numbers
A series of numbers developed by Fibonacci in which each number is the sum of the two preceding numbers. They are important because of their link to the 8:13 ratio: the golden section.

Symmetrical Grids

These two pages have symmetrical grids as the two pages are mirror images of each other. Thus the outer margin is the same on each page.

Flood colour
A term referring to the colour fill of an item.

Folio
A sheet of paper folded in half is a folio and each half of the folio is one page. A single folio has four pages.

Format
The shape and size of a book or page.

Gatefold
A page whereby the left and right edges fold inward with parallel folds and meet in the middle of the page without overlapping.

Golden section
A division in the ratio 8:13 that produces harmonious proportions.

Grid
A guide or template to help obtain design consistency.

Greeking
Nonsensical Latin words in a layout to give a visual representation of how the text will look. Also called dummy text.

Gutter
The space that comprises the fore or outer edge of a page, that is parallel to the back and the trim. The central alley-way where two pages meet at the spine, and the space between text columns is also referred to as the gutter.

Asymmetrical Grids

These pages use an asymmetrical grid as the grid of one page is exactly copied on the other page. Thus the left-hand margin is the same on each page.

Hanging or drop lines
A series of horizontal positioning lines that provide hook points for image and text block placement.

Head margin
The space at the top of the page; also called top margin.

Hierarchy
A logical, organised and visual guide for text headings indicating different levels of importance.

Horizontal alignment
The horizontal alignment of text in the field.

Hyphenation
The hyphen inserted at the point a word is broken in a justified text block.

Image
A photographic, diagrammatic or similar visual component.

Impart
The suggestion of ideas via the presention of information in a design. The viewer decodes this information to arrive at the required interpretation.

6pt Nonpareil
7pt Minion
8pt Brevier
9pt Bourgeois
10pt Long primer
12pt Pica
14pt English
16pt Great primer
20pt Paragon
24pt Two-line pica
28pt Double English

Point Sizes (British and American)

The British and American measurement of type size is based on a metric point; the dimensions of the point is 1/72 of an inch. All type is designated in points and, in turn, points are used to specify type size. There are 12 points to a pica (UK/US) and one pica is equal to 4.22mm.

Imposition
The arrangement of pages in the sequence and position in which they will appear when printed before being cut, folded and trimmed.

Imposition plan
A series of thumbnails of all the pages of a publication showing how it is laid out.

Indexing
Listed information in a contents page, index, glossary or contacts list.

Intensity
How crowded a design or spread is. A high-intensity design will contain a number of text and image elements. A low-intensity design will have lots of space incorporated into the page.

International Paper Sizes (ISO)
A range of standard metric paper sizes.

Justified
Text that is extended across the measure and aligned on both left and right margins.

The cap height of a piece of text aligns with the top of the hanging line.

Hanging or Drop Lines

These lines provide hook points for image and text block placement.

Juxtaposition
The placement of contrasting images side by side.

Layout
The arrangement of text and images according to a plan and to provide the appearance of the printed page.

Letter spacing
The distance between the letters of a word.

Locking (to a grid)
Fixing text to the baseline grid so that the grid determines spacing between text lines.

Margin
The spaces surrounding a text block at the sides, top and bottom of a page.

Marginalia
Text matter that appears in the page margin.

Juxtaposition

Juxtaposition is an image placement approach whereby related or contrasting images are placed side by side, such as a circle and a square.

Measure
The width in picas of a page or text column.

Module-based grid
A grid composed of an array of modules or fields, usually squares.

Orientation
The plane or direction in which text and images are used.

Orphan
A very short line comprised of a word (or the end of a hyphenated word) at the beginning of a paragraph or text column.

Page
A space in which to present images and text.

Pagination
The arrangement and numbering of pages in a publication.

Passe partout
A frame or border around an image or other element.

Passe Partout

Passe partout refers to the specific setting of an image so that it uses the white space of the edge of the page that surrounds it as a border.

Print finishing
Production processes undertaken to complete a printed work including, folding, binding and cutting.

Recto
The right-hand page of an open book.

Running heads
Repeated text that appears on each page of a work or section, also called header, running title or straplines.

Running shy
When there is insufficient material to fill a certain field or space.

Saddle-stitching
A binding method used for booklets, programmes and small catalogues. Signatures are nested and wire stitches are applied through the spine along the centrefold. When opened, saddle-stitched books lay flat.

Spot colour or special
A specially mixed colour used for printing.

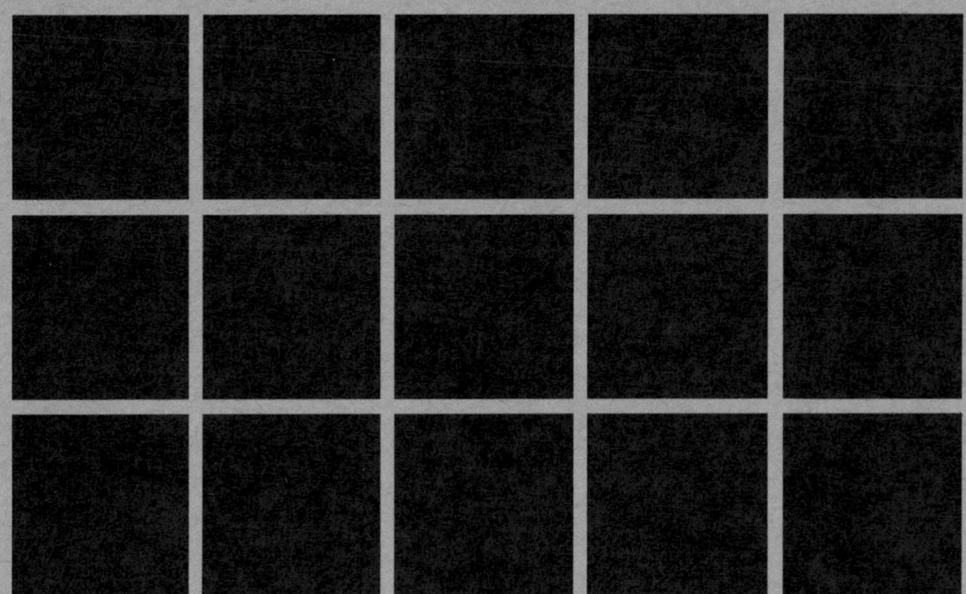

Modules or Fields

A module or field refers to one of a series of blocks that are used to construct a grid within which a design is created. Pictured above is a grid that comprises 15 modules.

Stock
The paper to be printed upon.

Structure
The skeleton to which elements on a page are positioned.

Substrate
The material or surface to be printed upon.

Swatch
A bolt-held book of colour or material samples.

Symmetrical grid
Grids on recto and verso pages that mirror one another.

Tip-in
To attach an inset in a book or magazine by gluing along the binding edge such as to tip-in a colour plate.

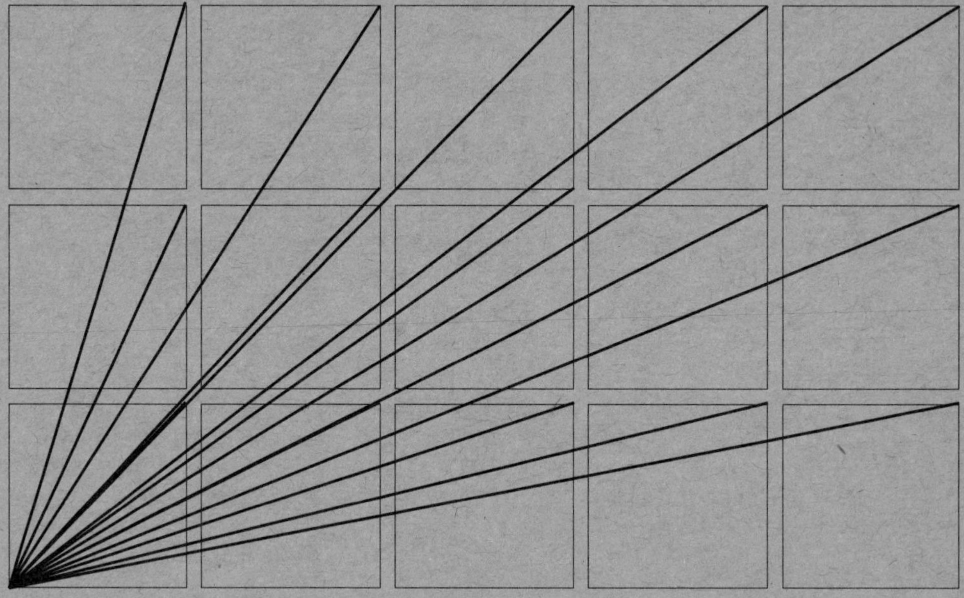

Possibilities

A module-based grid provides numerous image placement possibilities. Just by fixing an image to the bottom left corner of the grid there are 15 different image positions.

There are hundreds of different placement possibilities that can be found within this grid, ranging from the use of one module to incorporating all of them.

Verso
The left-hand page of an open book.

Vertical alignment
The vertical alignment of text in the field.

Widow
A very short line comprised of a word (or the end of a hyphenated word) at the end of a paragraph or text column.

Word spacing
The distance between words.

X-height
The height of lower case letters such as 'x' with no ascenders or descenders.

Z-bind
A 'z' shaped cover that is used to join two separate publications.

Conclusion

This book has outlined the basic layout concepts used by designers on a daily basis. This has included the use of various grids, columns and modules to provide a structure for the positioning of elements on the page. Different job specifications can place different requirements on the layout design depending upon the formats and finishing techniques used. Designs will instil emotions into the material they present via the use of space, the juxtaposition of elements and other techniques as the examples collected together in this volume illustrate. A thorough understanding of these concepts, together with knowledge of typography, format, colour and image, equips the designer with powerful tools to unleash tremendous creativity.

Design is a commercial pursuit and these basic principles facilitate the efficient use of design time whilst keeping costs within budget. Inspiration is the heart of creative activity and we hope that the commercial projects from leading contemporary design studios that illustrate this volume inspire you. We would like to give special thanks to everyone that has contributed work to make *Basics Design: Layout* such a visual treat.

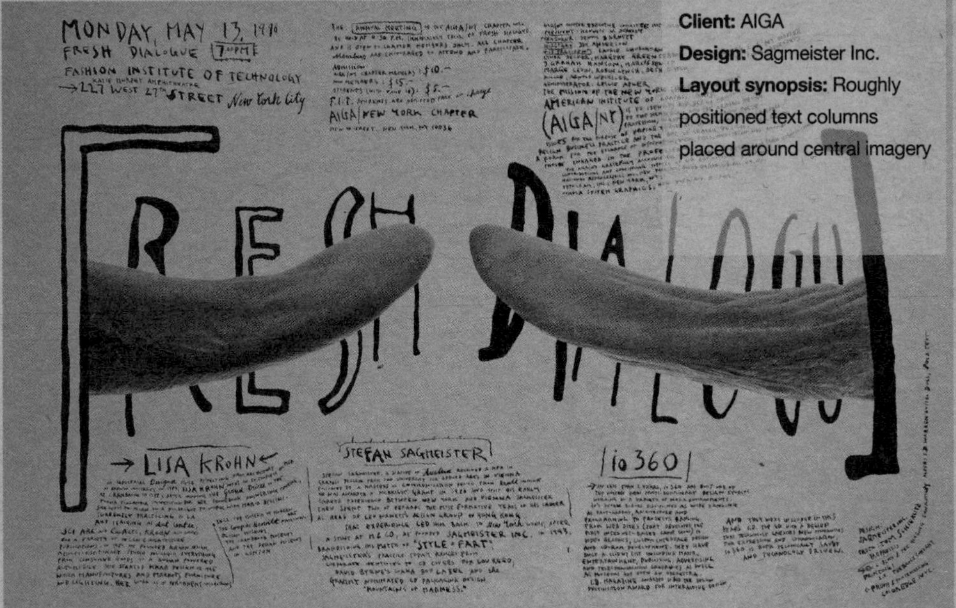

Client: AIGA

Design: Sagmeister Inc.

Layout synopsis: Roughly positioned text columns placed around central imagery

Fresh Dialogue

Stefan Sagmeister designed this poster for an American Institute of Graphic Art's (AIGA) conference. Handwritten typography, a hallmark of Stefan Sagmeister's work, is coupled with the seemingly haphazard placement of text blocks and images. However, the use of layout principles can be seen as the text is arranged in rough columns that support the imagery.

The tongues in the design represent the discussion that one assumes the conference will encourage amongst the delegates, though these wagging beauties are not saying much that would make sense to most as photographer Tom Schierlitz used cow tongues for the shoot.

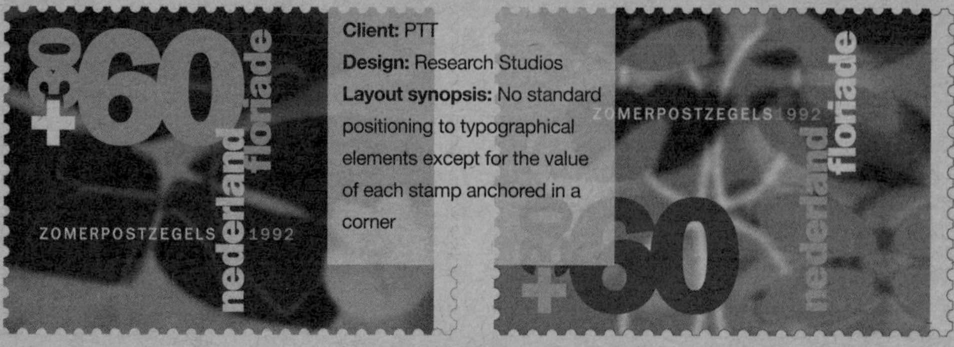

Client: PTT
Design: Research Studios
Layout synopsis: No standard positioning to typographical elements except for the value of each stamp anchored in a corner

PTT

Dutch telecommunications company PTT commissioned Research Studios to create a set of stamps that commemorated the quadrennial Floriade in 1992, the biggest flower show in the Netherlands.

The commission coincided with the first time the design studio had used Adobe Photoshop for image manipulation. The typographical elements are the same from stamp to stamp but positioned differently every time, maintaining a loose cross effect. Predominance is given to the value of each stamp, which is anchored in one of the corners.

Acknowledgements

We would like to thank everyone who supported us during the project, including the many art directors, designers and creatives who showed great generosity in allowing us to reproduce their work. Special thanks to everyone that hunted for, collated, compiled and rediscovered some of the fascinating work contained in this book. Thanks to Xavier Young for his patience, determination and skill in photographing the work showcased in this book and to Heather Marshall for modelling. And a final big thanks to Caroline Walmsley, Laura Owen, Brian Morris and all the staff at AVA Publishing who never tired of our requests, enquiries and questions, and supported us throughout.

Contacts

Agency	Contact	Page number
3 Deep Design	www.3deep.com.au	44, 66–67, 70
Aboud Sodano	www.aboud-sodano.com	86–87
Aufuldish + Warinner	www.aufwar.com	88–89, 126–127
Bis	www.bisdixit.com	105
Browns	www.brownsdesign.com	14–15, 132–133
Build	www.designbybuild.com	3
Cartlidge Levene	www.cartlidgelevene.co.uk	42–43, 97
Faydherbe / De Vringer	www.ben-wout.nl	30–31, 56–57, 125
Form Design	www.form.uk.com	62, 77, 84–85, 101, 139
Frost Design	www.frostdesign.co.uk	45, 104, 108–109, 129, 158–159
Gavin Ambrose	www.gavinambrose.co.uk	20–23, 79–81, 143
George & Vera	www.georgeandvera.com	85, 144–145, 157
Imagination	www.imagination.com	107, 140
Intro	www.intro-uk.com	120
KesselsKramer	www.kesselskramer.com	128, 131, 136, 152–153
NB: Studio	www.nbstudio.co.uk	34–35, 50–51, 72–73, 100, 106
North	www.northdesign.co.uk	16–17, 38–39, 46–47, 64–65, 91–93, 96, 111–113, 122–123
Research Studios	www.researchstudios.com	90–91, 146–147, 174
Rose Design	www.rosedesign.co.uk	98–99, 114–115
Roundel	www.roundel.com	61, 134–135, 141, 150–151
Sagmeister Inc.	www.sagmeister.com	173
SEA Design	www.seadesign.co.uk	19, 116–117, 132
Segura Inc.	www.segura-inc.com	10–11, 147
Spin	www.spin.co.uk	59, 71, 82–83, 124
Studio Myerscough	www.studiomyerscough.co.uk	52–53, 94–95, 102–103, 137–139, 153–155, 158
Thirteen	www.thirteen.co.uk	118–119, 121
Webb & Webb	www.webbandwebb.co.uk	7
Why Not Associates	www.whynotassociates.com	58, 78, 148–149